IT'S ALL ABOUT Baby

A Leisure Arts Publication by
Nancy M. Hill of

Acknowledgments

ACKNOWLEDGMENTS

©2003 by Leisure Arts, Inc., P. O. Box 55595, Little Rock, AR 72215. All rights reserved. This publication is protected under federal copyright laws. Reproduction or distribution of this publication or any other Leisure Arts publication, including publications that are out of print, is prohibited unless specifically authorized. This includes, but is not limited to, any form of reproduction on or through the Internet, including, posting, scanning, or e-mail transmission.

We have made every effort to ensure that these instruments are accurate and complete. We cannot, however, be responsible for human error, typographical mistakes, or variations in individual work.

It's All About Baby is the second in a series of books written by NanC and Company and published by Leisure Arts, Inc.

Author: Nancy M. Hill
Graphic Artist: Ty Thompson
Design Director: Candice Snyder
Assistant to Director: Candice Smoot
Cover Design: Maren Ogden &
 Miriam DeRosier
Copy Editor: Dr. Sharon Staples

For information about sales visit the Leisure Arts web site at www.leisurearts.com

It's All About Baby

Nana & Sydnee

THERE IS VERY LITTLE IN THIS WORLD THAT PARALLELS THE JOY THAT A YOUNG CHILD CAN BRING INTO OUR LIVES. WITH WONDER AND AWE I HAVE GAZED ADORINGLY AT A BRAND NEW BABY AND HAVE MARVELED AT MY CHILD AND THE MIRACLE OF BIRTH. I HAVE COUNTED FINGERS AND TOES AND KISSED LITTLE ROUND CHEEKS AND BUTTON NOSES. I HAVE WAITED EAGERLY FOR THAT FIRST SMILE, LAUGH AND GIGGLE. AND, OF COURSE, IF I COULD DO IT OVER AGAIN, I WOULD NEVER HAVE CHILDREN, ONLY GRANDCHILDREN, AND THEY WOULD BE ALLOWED TO TAKE A BATH IN 'NANA'S' KITCHEN SINK ANYTIME THEY WISHED!

IT HAS BEEN SAID THAT OF ALL THE BOOKS WE CAN GIVE OUR CHILDREN, THE ONE THEY WILL TREASURE THE MOST WILL BE THE ONE ABOUT THEM. GATHERING PHOTOS AND PAGES FOR THIS LATEST IDEA BOOK HAS BEEN A FUN PROJECT FOR ALL OF US IN THE DESIGN OFFICE. HOW COULD WE NOT HAVE FUN BEING SURROUNDED BY HAPPY BABY PHOTOS AND SCRAPBOOK PAGES FOR THE PAST THREE MONTHS?

AS WE GATHERED PHOTOS, CREATED PAGES, AND REVIEWED SUBMISSIONS FROM DESIGNERS, I FOUND MYSELF FOCUSING NOT ONLY ON THE PAGES, TECHNIQUES, PHOTOGRAPHY AND JOURNALING, BUT ALSO ON THE LOVED ONES BEHIND THE CAMERA. I THOUGHT OF THOSE WHO STAGED OR CAPTURED THE SHOTS, DRESSED THE CHILD, DEVELOPED THE FILM, AND SAVED THE MOMENT FOREVER WITH A SCRAPBOOK PAGE. I FOCUSED ON THEIR LOVE OF THE CHILD AND INTEREST IN PRESERVING A MEMORY AND CREATING SOMETHING MEMORABLE FOR THE CHILD TO LOOK BACK UPON AND KNOW THEY WERE LOVED.

IT'S ALL ABOUT BABY IS FULL OF GREAT IDEAS TO HELP YOU CREATE MEMORABLE PAGES. THIS IDEA BOOK HAS BEEN DESIGNED SO YOU CAN DO SOME SERIOUS "PAGE LIFTING." WE HAVE INCLUDED DETAILED DESCRIPTIONS OF PAGE CONSTRUCTION THAT CAN BE EASILY DUPLICATED.

MAY YOU FIND JOY IN CAPTURING MEMORIES OF THE BABIES IN YOUR LIFE,

Nancy

NANCY M. HILL

Table of Contents

Birth Day

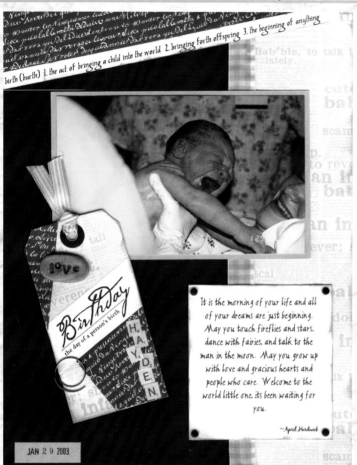

Designer: Brandy A. Logan

JAN 2 9 2003

It is the morning of your life and all of your dreams are just beginning. May you touch fireflies and stars, dance with fairies, and talk to the man in the moon. May you grow up with love and gracious hearts and people who care. Welcome to the world little one, its been waiting for you.

~April Hardwick

BIRTHDAY

• CREATE BACKGROUND BY ADHERING STRIP OF BABY BLUE PAPER, BLACK WORD PAPER AND BLUE GINGHAM RIBBON TO BLACK TEXTURED CARDSTOCK • MAT PHOTO WITH CARDSTOCK AND ADHERE TO BACKGROUND • PRINT JOURNALING ON CARDSTOCK • ATTACH JOURNALING BLOCK WITH FOUR BLACK BRADS • ADHERE DEFINITION TO LAYOUT • CREATE TAG USING SCRAPS OF PAPER • ADHERE 'BIRTHDAY' DEFINITION • CUT OUT BABY'S NAME USING SCRABBLE LETTER PAPER AND ADHERE TO TAG • CREATE BLACK CIRCLE FOR TAG USING CIRCLE PUNCH AND HOLE PUNCH • T[…] RIBBON THROUGH TAG'S HOLE AND TRIM • EMBELLISH TAG WITH CIRCLE CLIP AND CLAY LOVE PEBBLE AND ADHERE TO LAYOUT • STAMP DATE ON SCRAP PIECE OF CARDSTOCK AND ADHERE TO BACKGROUND • INK EDGES OF PAPER, JOURNALING BLOCK, TAG AND DEFINITIONS WITH INK •

SUPPLIES – CARDSTOCK: BAZZILL; PATTERNED PAPER: 7 GYPSIES; INK: CLEARSNAP; CLAY: SCULPEY; STAMP: HERO ARTS; PUNCH: FAMILY TREASURES; DEFINITION TITLE: MAKING MEMORIES; BRADS: AMERICAN TAG; CIRCLE CLIP: MAKING MEMORIES; FONT: TWO PEAS IN A BUCKET BLISSFUL

SPECIAL TIPS:

1. USE A PRE-MADE TAG AS A GUIDE TO MAKE AN EASY CUSTOM TAG. GLUE SEVERAL PAPERS RANDOMLY TO THE TOP AND TRIM AWAY THE EXCESS.
2. MAKE CLAY PEBBLES BY STAMPING DESIGNS AND BAKING AS DIRECTED.

REMEMBER THIS

• BEGIN WITH BLACK CARDSTOCK FOR BACKGROUND • TEAR PHOTO MAT AND PAINT WITH DRY BRUSH TECHNIQUE • MAT PHOTO WITH DRY MAT AND ADHERE TO BACKGROUND • FRAME PHOTO WITH LABELS • FRAME ACCENT PHOTO WITH METAL FRAME • RUB-ON TITLE • STAMP DESIGN WITH FOAM RUBBER STAMP AND ACRYLIC PAINT • ATTACH GINGHAM RIBBON TO LAYOUT WITH STAPLES • ADHERE FRAMED PHOTO WITH METAL GLUE • EMBELLISH WITH METAL PHOTO CORNERS •

SUPPLIES – CARDSTOCK: BAZZILL; STAMP: MICHAEL'S; METAL FRAME: MAKING MEMORIES; TITLE: MAKING MEMORIES; PHOTO CORNERS: MAKING MEMORIES; LABEL MAKER: DYMO

SPECIAL TIPS:

USE A DRY BRUSH TECHNIQUE WHEN USING ACRYLIC PAINTS ON CARDSTOCK. IF THE PAPER WARPS FROM TOO MUCH PAINT, PRESS THE BACKSIDE OF THE CARDSTOCK WITH AN IRON AFTER THE PAINT IS DRY.

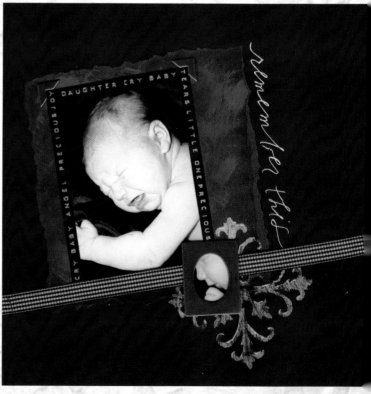

remember this

Baby Girl

• CREATE BACKGROUND PAPER BY PRINTING DESCRIPTIVE WORDS IN UPPER AND LOWER CASE • ADHERE COLORED CARDSTOCKS TO PRINTED PAPER • CHANGE BACKGROUND OF BABY PHOTO TO BLACK AND WHITE AND ADD BABY'S NAME TO PHOTO • PRINT OUT PHOTO IN BLACK AND WHITE • ATTACH STICKERS FOR TITLE • PRINT AND CUT OUT DATE AND JOURNALING • TEAR EDGES OF JOURNALING AND ADHERE TO THREE TAGS • ATTACH EYELETS TO EACH TAG AND THREAD WITH WHITE CHENILLE FIBER • CREATE COVER PAGE OF STORY BOOK WITH DESCRIPTIVE WORD PAPER, TEXTURED CARDSTOCK AND MINI PHOTO • CREATE BOOK BY FOLDING A PIECE OF PAPER, INSERTING COVER AND FILLER PAGES AND ATTACHING WITH STAR EYELETS • CUT OUT TWO THIN STRIPS OF CARDSTOCK AND ATTACH TO BACKGROUND WITH BRADS • PENETRATE SURFACE ABOVE STRIPS WITH AN EXACTO KNIFE AND INSERT TAGS • ADHERE THIRD TAG WITH A VELLUM ENVELOPE •

SUPPLIES – CARDSTOCK: BAZZILL; EYELETS: MAKING MEMORIES; STICKERS: SONNET'S; FONT: SCRIPTINA, TWO PEAS IN A BUCKET NEVERMIND, TWO PEAS IN A BUCKET SHACK, TWO PEAS IN A BUCKET SHACK WIDE, TWO PEAS IN A BUCKET COOKIE DOUGH; TWO PEAS IN A BUCKET CHESTNUTS

Benjamin

• CREATE BACKGROUND BY CUTTING OUT A LARGE SQUARE IN THE CENTER OF PATTERNED PAPER, ADHERING BLUE CARDSTOCK ATOP THE BORDER PIECE AND ADHERING CUT OUT PIECE ATOP THE BLUE CARDSTOCK • ENLARGE AND PRINT PHOTO • CREATE TITLE WITH METAL LETTERS • ATTACH TO BACKGROUND WITH SILVER EYELETS AND FIBERS • PRINT QUOTE ON TRANSPARENCY AND CUT TO FIT PHOTO • EMBELLISH LAYOUT WITH BRADS, LETTER BEAD CHAIN, AND STICKERS •

SUPPLIES – PRINTED PAPER: LEISURE ARTS; EYELET LETTERS: MAKING MEMORIES; BLOCK LETTERS: LEISURE ARTS; BRADS: MAKING MEMORIES; FIBER: FIBERS BY THE YARD; STICKERS: KANGAROO & JOEY

SPECIAL TIP:
PLACE A SPECIAL EMPHASIS ON WORDS BY USING BEADS OR LETTER STICKERS.

IT'S ALL ABOUT
The Lullaby

Designer: Jan Cousins

Our bundle of joy!

Ben·6weeks

BUNDLE OF JOY

• CREATE BACKGROUND BY ADHERING TORN STRIPS OF YELLOW PAPER TO BLUE PATTERNED PAPER • MAT PHOTO WITH WHITE CARDSTOCK • PRINT TITLE ONTO A TRANSPARENCY AND ADHERE TO BACK-GROUND WITH SCRAPPERS SPRAY • WRAP FIBER AROUND LAYOUT • ATTACH BABY CHARMS • ADHERE BUTTONS • OUTLINE PHOTO AND LAYOUT WITH PEN • SUPPLIES – PAPER: LEISURE ARTS; CHARMS: LEISURE ARTS; FIBER: FIBERS BY THE YARD; BUTTONS: MAKING MEMORIES; FONT: P22 CEZANNE

SPECIAL TIPS:
1. HANDWRITE ONTO A TRANSPARENCY FOR AN EASY ALTERNATIVE TO HAND-WRITING DIRECTLY ONTO A PAGE. IF A MISTAKE IS MADE, JUST REPRINT.
2. BUTTONS MAKE A NICE EMBELLISH-MENT AND ARE EASY TO FIND.

3

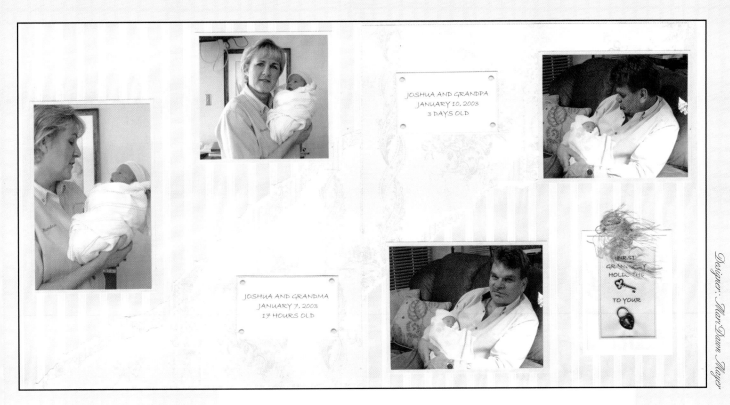

Grandpa and Grandma

• CREATE BACKGROUND BY ADHERING DIAGONALLY RIPPED PATTERNED PAPERS TO A COORDINATING PATTERNED PAPER • MAT AND ADHERE PHOTOS • MAT PRINTED JOURNALING AND ATTACH WITH BRADS • PRINT TAG JOURNALING ON VELLUM • TRIPLE MAT WITH PATTERNED PAPER AND CARDSTOCK • EMBELLISH WITH FIBERS AND CHARMS • Supplies — Patterned Paper: Anna Griffin; Brads: Doodlebug

Sydnee and Isaac

• BEGIN WITH GREEN PATTERNED PAPER FOR BACKGROUND • MAT PHOTOS WITH GREEN AND BLUE CARDSTOCK • BABY STAMP MATS WITH A WATERMARK PAD • CREATE TITLE BY ATTACHING LETTER STICKERS TO BUTTONS AND ADHERING TO LAYOUT WITH GLUE DOTS • ATTACH LETTER STICKERS TO BLUE AND YELLOW CARDSTOCK TO FINISH TITLE • EMBELLISH LAYOUT WITH STICKERS AND BUTTONS ATTACHED WITH EMBROIDERY FLOSS • Supplies — Patterned Paper: Leisure Arts; Stamp: Imagination; Stickers: Leisure Arts

IT'S ALL ABOUT

Sleep

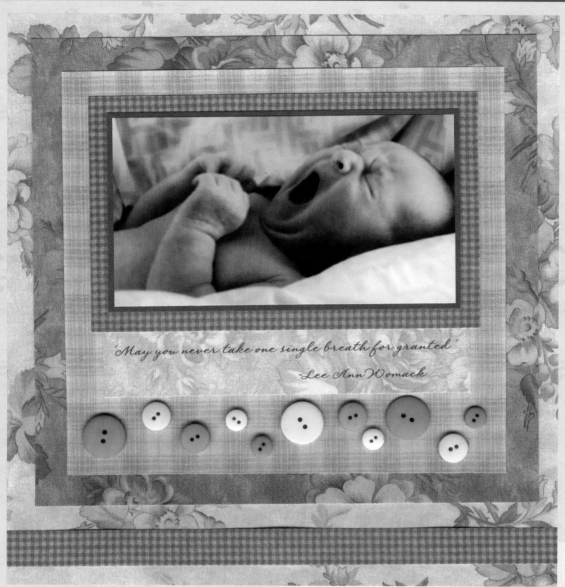

'May you never take one single breath for granted'
-Lee Ann Womack

Designer: Tammy Mellish

MAY YOU NEVER TAKE ONE SINGLE BREATH FOR GRANTED

• CREATE BACKGROUND BY ADHERING TWO SQUARES OF COORDINATING PAPER TO A FLOWER PATTERNED PAPER • CHANGE BLACK AND WHITE PHOTO TO SEPIA AND ENLARGE CROPPED PHOTO TO 5X7 • MAT PHOTO WITH TEXTURED CARDSTOCK AND GINGHAM PAPER • PRINT LYRICS FROM LEE ANN WOMACK'S SONG ONTO PATTERNED PAPER • ADHERE MATED PHOTO AND LYRICS TO PAGE • RANDOMLY ADHERE BUTTONS WITH GLUE DOTS • EMBELLISH WITH RIBBON •
SUPPLIES – PATTERNED PAPER: DAISY D'S, BAZZILL; CARDSTOCK: BAZZILL; BUTTONS: MAKING MEMORIES

5

Dream

- CREATE BACKGROUND FROM TORN PIECES OF CARD-STOCK • PRINT PHOTO ONTO CARDSTOCK USING COMPUTER • MAT PHOTO WITH CARDSTOCK AND MULBERRY PAPER USING POP DOTS • ADHERE TO BACKGROUND • USE STAMPS TO CREATE TITLE • EMBELLISH WITH FIBERS, BUTTONS AND PAGE PEBBLES •

SUPPLIES – PAPER: CAROLEE'S CREATIONS; CARDSTOCK: BAZZILL; FIBER: FIBER ACCENTS; BUTTONS: JESSE JAMES & COMPANY; STAMPS: ANITA'S, HERO ARTS; PEBBLES: MAKING MEMORIES

Designer: Wendi Speciale

Photo Manipulation

Photo manipulation can completely change the look of a scrapbooking page. There are endless ways to manipulate your photo, so be creative and have fun. Here are some ideas!

- Enlarge a photo and print two copies. Use different sized square punches to punch out different areas of one photo. Adhere the squares raised atop the uncut photo with double-sided foam tape or pop dots. Place the squares over the same part of the uncut photo.
- Elongate a photo by cutting it into strips and adhering it to a layout with space in between each strip. Add dimension by matting strips with corrugated cardboard.
- Partially cover a photo with a torn piece of vellum. Text can even be printed onto the vellum for a different look.
- Adhere a series of action photos to add motion and excitement to your layout.
- Laminate photos with transparent colors using a Xyron machine. Change the mood of a layout by laminating copies of the same photo with different colors.
- Partially cover a photo with mesh and attach to photo with a brad, eyelet or other embellishment.

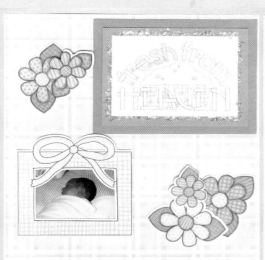

Sweet Dreams

- CREATE BACKGROUND BY MATTING TRIMMED PATTERNED PAPER TO PINK PATTERNED CARDSTOCK • ADHERE PHOTOS TO PAPER FRAMES • DOUBLE MAT TITLE AND JOURNALING WITH CARDSTOCK AND GLITTER • EMBELLISH WITH FLOWER STICKERS •

YOU

blue
eyes

happy

BOY

Designer: Sam Cousins

OUR POT OF GOLD
• CREATE BACKGROUND BY ADHERING
TORN STRIPED PAPER TO YELLOW
CHECKED PAPER • ADHERE PHOTO
AND ATTACH LETTER STICKERS FOR
TITLE • WRAP FEATHER FIBER AROUND
ENTIRE LAYOUT • OUTLINE PHOTO
AND LAYOUT WITH PEN •
SUPPLIES – PATTERNED PAPER: LEISURE
ARTS; STICKERS: FLAVIA; FIBER: FIBERS BY
THE YARD

SPECIAL TIPS:
DRAW A LINED BORDER WITH A
FINE-TIPPED PEN TO ADD DEFINI-
TION TO PHOTOS AND LAYOUTS.

YOU
• BEGIN WITH YELLOW CHECKED PAPER FOR
BACKGROUND • PRINT PHOTO IN PANORAMIC
SETTING • TEAR DARK STRIPED PAPER AND
ADHERE TO BACKGROUND WITH PHOTO SHOW-
ING THROUGH THE TEAR • ATTACH VARIOUS
STICKERS AND WORDS DESCRIBING THE BABY TO
THE DARK PAPER • ADHERE FUN FIBER AROUND
DARK PAPER USING A TWO-WAY GLUE PEN •
SUPPLIES – PATTERNED PAPER: LEISURE ARTS;
STICKERS: LEISURE ARTS, SONNETS, SEI, RENAE
LINDGREN, MAKING MEMORIES, KINKADE; FIBER:
FIBERS BY THE YARD; BRADS: MAKING MEMORIES;
EYELET LETTERS: MAKING MEMORIES

SPECIAL TIPS:
DON'T ALWAYS PRINT YOUR PHOTOS
IN TRADITIONAL 3X5 OR 4X6 FOR-
MATS. PRINT LARGE OR PANORAMIC
PHOTOS FOR VARIETY.

our POT of GOLD

Ben, you had such a good time at Sherwood's Pumpkin Patch. You rode around in your little red wagon & picked out your very first pumpkin October 2002

PUMPKIN PATCH KID

• CREATE BACKGROUND BY ADHERING TORN PIECES OF DENIM PAPER TO GREEN CARDSTOCK • FRAME SMALL PHOTO WITH DENIM PHOTO FRAME • TIE DENIM RIBBON AROUND PICTURE FRAME • CUT STRIPES FROM TAG SQUARE SHEET AND ATTACH TO TWO SIDES OF A PHOTO WITH BRADS • USE BEIGE CENTER FROM PHOTO FRAME AND ADHERE TO INSIDE OF DENIM TAG SQUARE FOR TITLE • PRINT TITLE ON TRANSPARENCY AND ATTACH WITH BRADS • ATTACH TWO EYELETS AND STRING DENIM RIBBON THROUGH • ATTACH 'MY FIRST PUMPKIN' METAL TAG TO THE LAYOUT • EMBELLISH WITH BRADS •
SUPPLIES – PATTERNED PAPER: LEISURE ARTS; FONT: BATIK

BEN OCTOBER 2003

• CREATE BACKGROUND BY ADHERING A BLUE PATTERNED PAPER WITH TORN AND CHALKED EDGES TO THE OUTER PIECE OF A BROWN PAPER WITH CENTER CUT OUT • CRUMPLE, SAND, AND INK OUTER AND CENTER PIECE OF CUT BROWN PAPER • FRAME TWO PHOTOS WITH DISTRESSED STICKER FRAMES • ADHERE PHOTOS TO BROWN SQUARE • USE THE CENTER OF ONE FRAME AS THE TITLE BACKGROUND • PRINT TITLE ON TRANSPARENCY • ADHERE FIBER UNDER TITLE AND ACROSS PAGE • ATTACH TITLE ELEMENTS TO BACKGROUND WITH BRADS • TWIST AND ATTACH WIRE TO TITLE • CUT CENTER FROM OTHER FRAME INTO STRIPS • PRINT NAME AND DATE ONTO STRIPS AND ADHERE TO THE PHOTOS • PUNCH PHOTOS OF PUMPKINS WITH SQUARE PUNCH AND ADHERE WITH POP-DOTS OVER FIBER •
SUPPLIES – PAPER: LEISURE ARTS; FRAMES: LEISURE ARTS; FIBER: FIBERS BY THE YARD

SPECIAL TIPS:

1. SAND, CRINKLE, INK AND TEAR YOUR PAPER TO GIVE IT A DISTRESSED LOOK.
2. USE ALL YOUR SCRAPS. THE PUMPKIN SQUARES WERE FROM CUT UP PHOTOS AND THE TITLE BLOCK AND STRIPS INSIDE THE FRAMES WERE FROM THE INSETS OF THE FRAMES.
3. IF YOU ARE USING MULTIPLE PIECES OF PAPER FOR THE BACKGROUND, CUT THE CENTER OUT OF THE BOTTOM PIECE (IT CANNOT BE SEEN BECAUSE THE OTHER SHEET WILL HIDE IT) AND IT CAN BE USED LATER ON THE SAME LAYOUT OR FOR ANOTHER PURPOSE.

IT'S ALL ABOUT
Little Girls

KRYSTAL

Sweetest Thing

- CREATE BACKGROUND BY ADHERING TORN PATTERNED PAPER TO CARDSTOCK • MAT PHOTO WITH PATTERNED PAPER AND CARDSTOCK • CREATE TITLE WITH LETTER STICKERS • FRAME POEM STICKER WITH METAL FRAME • ADHERE CORRUGATED CARDBOARD ACROSS PAGE • WIND TULLE AROUND PHOTO AND ADHERE TO LAYOUT • EMBELLISH WITH HEARTS •

SUPPLIES – PATTERNED PAPER: PAPER ILLUZIONZ; HEARTS: SCRAPWORKS; METAL FRAME: MAKING MEMORIES

9

PRECIOUS McKINLEY

• CREATE BACKGROUND BY ADHERING TORN CARDSTOCK TO LIGHT BLUE CARDSTOCK • ATTACH PHOTO TO BACKGROUND WITH METAL PHOTO CORNERS • PRINT JOURNALING ONTO LARGE TAG AND INSERT INTO POCKET • ADHERE EYELET WORDS • STAMP DESIGN WITH FOAM RUBBER STAMP AND ACRYLIC METALLIC PAINT • PUNCH HOLES IN LAYOUT AND THREAD WITH FIBERS TIED IN BOWS • EMBELLISH POCKET WITH FIBERS, STAMP AND CHARM •
SUPPLIES: CARDSTOCK: BAZZILL; FIBER: BROWN BAG FIBERS, TIMELESS TOUCHES; EYELET WORDS: MAKING MEMORIES; PHOTO CORNERS: MAKING MEMORIES; TAG: FOOFALA

LOVE BUG

• CREATE BACKGROUND BY ADHERING A PIECE OF PATTERNED PAPER AND PINK SPLATTER NET TO PINK CARDSTOCK • DOUBLE MAT PHOTO • CREATE TITLE BY STRINGING METAL LETTER BLOCKS ON FIBERS • ATTACH OVER SPLATTER NET WITH BRADS • ATTACH STICKER LETTERS TO FINISH THE TITLE • PRINT JOURNALING ON CLEAR VELLUM AND TEAR LOWER EDGE • CUT FIBERS AND ATTACH TO JOURNALING BLOCK AND LAYOUT WITH BRAD • CREATE TAG BY MATTING A PUNCHED SQUARE OF PATTERNED PAPER WITH WHITE AND PURPLE CARDSTOCKS • ATTACH FIBERS TO TAG AND LAYOUT WITH TWO SILVER MINI BRADS • EMBELLISH LAYOUT WITH FLOWER STICKERS AND CHARMS • OUTLINE LAYOUT WITH WATERCOLOR PENCILS AND BLACK MARKER •
SUPPLIES – PATTERNED PAPER: LEISURE ARTS; NETTING: SCRAPLOVERS; METAL LETTER BLOCKS: LEISURE ARTS; STICKERS: LEISURE ARTS; CHARMS: LEISURE ARTS; FIBER: FIBERS BY THE YARD; VELLUM: PAPER ADVENTURES; SILVER BRADS: ALL THE EXTRAS; PURPLE BRADS: MAKING MEMORIES; LETTER STICKERS: BEARY PATCH

IT'S ALL ABOUT
Little Girls

Jiulia is so lovely in her beautiful Christening dress.
The dress was given to Jiulia by her God Mother, Rosie Brito.
These photos were taken on Jiulia's first birthday.
Her Christening was performed when she was 9 months old.

First
Birthday

June 14th
2003

Jiulia

JIULIA

• CREATE BACKGROUND BY ADHERING TRIMMED PATTERNED PAPER TO RED CARDSTOCK •
DOUBLE MAT PHOTOS WITH PINK VELLUM AND CARDSTOCK • CREATE TITLE BY ADHERING
ALPHABET STICKERS TO 1" SQUARES OF PINK VELLUM MATTED WITH CARDSTOCK • PRINT
JOURNALING ON VELLUM • ADHERE TITLE TO BACKGROUND OVER RED THREAD WITH KNOTS
ON BOTH SIDES • WRAP JOURNALING WITH THREAD AND ADHERE TO BACKGROUND • MAT
FLORAL STICKER BORDERS WITH CARDSTOCK • ADHERE BORDERS TO LAYOUT •
SUPPLIES — PATTERNED PAPER: LEISURE ARTS; STICKERS: LEISURE ARTS; FIBER: TWOTWINKLES.COM

Luv Made Visible

- BEGIN WITH PINK CARDSTOCK BACKGROUND • MAT PICTURE WITH PATTERNED PAPERS • PRINT AND MAT JOURNALING • CREATE TITLE BY STRINGING BEADS AND LETTERS ON WIRE • ATTACH WIRED BEADS BELOW PHOTO • HANG HANDWRITTEN TAG FROM WIRE USING SAFETY PIN • EMBELLISH JOURNALING WITH SAFETY PIN AND WIRED BEADS •

SUPPLIES – PATTERNED PAPER: LEISURE ARTS; METAL LETTERS: LEISURE ARTS

Kelly Mieko

- CREATE BACKGROUND BY ADHERING PATTERNED VELLUM TO ROSE CARDSTOCK WITH VELLUM TAPE • DOUBLE MAT PICTURES WITH CARDSTOCK • TEAR BOTTOM EDGE OF ONE MAT AND CHALK TORN EDGE • PRINT TITLE ONTO VELLUM AND MAT WITH CARDSTOCK • TEAR AND CHALK EDGES AND ADHERE TO PAGE • CUT TAG WITH TEMPLATE • SHADE TAG WITH CHALKS • ATTACH EYELET, RIBBON, AND PAPER WOVEN LACE TO TAG • ADHERE TO LAYOUT • CUT MATCHING STRIPS OF CARDSTOCK AND WEAVE IN ECRU LACE • DAB ENDS OF LACE WITH TACKY GLUE TO PREVENT FRAYING • ADHERE LACE TO BACKGROUND WITH GLUE DOTS • EMBELLISH WITH BUTTONS AND STICKERS •

SUPPLIES – CARDSTOCK: MAKING MEMORIES, CREATIVE MEMORIES; PRINTED VELLUM: AUTUMN LEAVES; BUTTONS: DRESS IT UP; TAG: DELUXE CUTS; EYELETS: DOODLEBUG; FONT: TWO PEAS IN A BUCKET BEAUTIFUL

IT'S ALL ABOUT
Little Boys

Human
beings
can create

all manner
of Things
to bring
joy
But only a

Wonderful
G O D
could have
created a
Beautiful little
boy

C O R E Y

Designer: Tammy Saud

SPECIAL TIPS:
SPEED UP DRYING TIME BY
USING AN EMBOSSING GUN.

COREY

• BEGIN WITH PLAID PAPER FOR BACKGROUND • WET AND CRUMPLE LIGHT BLUE
CARDSTOCK • LAY FLAT TO DRY • DOUBLE MAT PHOTO WITH CRUMPLED PAPER AND
SANDED TAN PAPER • ADHERE BUTTONS, FIBERS AND TINY EYELETS TO PHOTO MAT •
HANDWRITE QUOTE MIXING IN STAMPED AND METAL LETTERS • CHALK WHITE TAGS
WITH BLUE AND BROWN CHALK • ATTACH SILVER LETTER STICKERS TO TAGS • ATTACH
TAGS TO LAYOUT WITH BRADS • ADHERE PICKET FENCE WITH GLUE DOTS •
SUPPLIES – PATTERNED PAPER: MAKING MEMORIES; CARDSTOCK: BAZZILL; STAMPS: STAMPIN'
UP; METAL LETTERS: MAKING MEMORIES; TAGS: MAKING MEMORIES, AVERY; BUTTONS:
DRESS IT UP; FENCE: WESTRIM CRAFTS

One Little Boy

• CREATE BACKGROUND BY ADHERING GREEN CRACKLED PAPER TO DENIM PAPER • CUT THREE SIDES OF A RECTANGLE (LEAVING THE TOP UNCUT) IN THE DENIM PAPER WITH A PAPER TRIMMER • ROLL UP CUT PAPER • ADHERE GREEN PAPER TO THE WHITE ROLL THAT IS LEFT SHOWING • TIE THE ROLL WITH STRING TO LOOK LIKE A WINDOW BLIND • ADHERE PHOTO BEHIND WINDOW • ADHERE OTHER PHOTO TO LAYOUT • FRAME PHOTO WITH STRIPS OF DENIM PAPER • ATTACH TO LAYOUT WITH A CROSS-STITCH IN EACH CORNER • PRINT TITLE AND JOURNALING ONTO CARDSTOCK AND ADHERE TO LAYOUT •

Supplies – Patterned Paper: Leisure Arts; Cardstock: Paper Garden; Computer Font: CK Rugged

Little boys' pockets
hold magical things,
Earthworms,
apple cores,
a mess of string.
But this treasure is nothing
to the wealth one finds
in little boys' hearts
and little boys' minds.
–author unknown

one little boy
–ocean in sept. 2003

Designer: Tori Anderson

Ty Joseph Booms
Aug. 1, 2003
6lbs 4oz

precious little one

Precious Little One

• CREATE BACKGROUND BY ADHERING BLUE CARDSTOCK TO GREEN CARDSTOCK • MAT PHOTO WITH CARDSTOCK AND ADHERE TO BACKGROUND • ATTACH RUB-ON WORDS TO STRIP OF CARDSTOCK FOR TITLE • PRINT JOURNALING ON WHITE CARDSTOCK • TEAR AND MAT WITH TORN CARDSTOCK AND ATTACH WITH PAPER CLIP AND STRING • CRUMPLE PATTERNED PAPER AND ADHERE TO LAYOUT OVERLAPPING PHOTO • ADHERE METAL FRAME LIKE A BUCKLE •

Supplies – Patterned Paper: Chatterbox; Cardstock: Bazzill; Frame: Making Memories; Title: Making Memories

IT'S ALL ABOUT
Little Boys

Aging Techniques

AGING PAPER IS A COMMON SCRAPBOOKING ACTIVITY. THE METHOD CAN TIE AN ENTIRE LAYOUT TOGETHER AND ANY SCRAPBOOKING ELEMENT CAN BE AGED (PAPER, PHOTOS, STICKERS, ACCENTS, FIBERS, ETC.). THE SCRAPBOOKER HAS A VARIETY OF AGING OPTIONS AVAILABLE TODAY.

WALNUT INK IS THE MOST POPULAR AGING MEDIUM AND WORKS VERY WELL. IT IS GREAT FOR STAINING, SPRAYING, BRUSHING AND TEXTURING PAPERS. WALNUT INK IS TAKEN FROM THE SHELLS OF WALNUTS AND COMES IN AN OILY, CRYSTALLIZED FORM. TO USE, JUST ADD WATER. THE COLOR OF THE STAIN DEPENDS ON HOW MUCH WATER IS USED (DARK—LESS WATER, LIGHT—MORE WATER). A QUICK AND EASY WAY TO AGE PAPER IS TO WET PAPER, CRUMPLE, AND DIP IT IN THE INK MIXTURE. LEAVE THE PAPER IN THE INK MIXTURE LONGER FOR A DARKER RESULT. IF THE RESULT IS TOO DARK, THE PAPER CAN BE RINSED. THE INK MIXTURE CAN ALSO BE BRUSHED ONTO PAPER WITH A FOAM BRUSH OR SPONGE. THERE ARE MANY WAYS TO USE THE INK SO EXPERIMENT AND HAVE FUN WITH IT. LET THE INK DRY BY SPREADING PAPER FLAT ON A TOWEL OR IRONING PAPER ON A COTTON SETTING. WALNUT INK WORKS GREAT ON MOST PAPERS, BUT THERE ARE SOME THAT DO NOT ABSORB THE INK.

ACRYLIC PAINT AND SANDING CAN GIVE AN AGED LOOK TO A VARIETY OF PRODUCTS. DRY BRUSH PAPER WITH ACRYLIC PAINT AND LET IT DRY. THEN SAND THE PAPER FOR AN AGED LOOK. SANDING, EVEN WITHOUT THE PAINT, WILL ADD YEARS TO A PRODUCT. JUST BE CAREFUL NOT TO SAND TOO HEARTILY!

TEA BAG DYING IS ANOTHER AGING OPTION. BOIL WATER IN A POT AND ADD A TEA BAG. STAIN PAPER IN A SIMILAR MANNER TO THE OTHER WATER BASED STAINS.

METALLIC AND LUSTER RUB-ONS ARE USED AS AN AGING MEDIUM AS WELL. THEY HAVE THE ADVANTAGE OF ADHERING TO MANY DIFFERENT MATERIALS. RUB-ONS WORK ESPECIALLY WELL ON METAL AND PAPER AND CAN BE BUFFED IF DESIRED. THEY ARE BEST APPLIED WITH A FINGER (COVERED WITH A LATEX GLOVE) OR RAG.

RUB N' BUFF IS ANOTHER RUB-ON MEDIUM WITH A WAX METALLIC FINISH. IT WORKS VERY WELL ON METAL AND IS LONG LASTING. RUB N' BUFF COMES IN A SMALL SQUEEZABLE TUBE AND IS BEST APPLIED WITH A FINGER AND BUFFED WITH A SOFT TOWEL.

AGING CHALKS WORK WELL ON MOST PAPERS AND ARE EASILY APPLIED WITH A COTTON SWAB OR MAKE-UP SPONGE.

FOLK ANTIQUING MEDIUM IS A WATER BASED STAIN USED ON WOOD AND PAPER ALIKE. IT COMES READY TO USE, BUT CAN BE WATERED DOWN FOR A LIGHTER WASH.

Designer: Peggy Manrique

LITTLE COWBOY

• CREATE BACKGROUND BY ADHERING STRIPED PAPER, BEIGE PAPER AND COLLAGE PAPER TO RED PAPER • TEAR, CRUMPLE, FLATTEN AND ADHERE TEXTURED LOFT PAPER TO BACKGROUND • PAINT EDGES OF PHOTOS WITH METALLIC RUB-ON AND ADHERE TO BACKGROUND • WEAVE STRING THROUGH TAG LETTER STICKERS FOR TITLE AND KNOT THE ENDS • ADHERE TITLE TO LAYOUT • STRING RAFFIA THROUGH DATE TAGS AND ADHERE TO LAYOUT WITH KNOTS IN CORNERS TO FRAME PHOTO • MAKE PAGE ACCENT WITH COLLAGE PAPER, WISDOM LEATHER, STICKERS AND TINY BUTTONS • ATTACH THE 'J' TAG WITH A SAFETY PIN AND GLUE DOTS • USE A METAL TAG RIM TO FRAME THE AGE OF THE BABY •

Supplies – Patterned Paper: Chatterbox, Paper Loft, Legacy Collage; Metal Rim: Making Memories; Metal Tag: Making Memories; Stickers: Nostalgique

SPECIAL TIPS:

1. STRING LETTER STICKERS WHILE STILL ATTACHED TO THE STICKER PAPER.
2. CHALK OR METALLIC RUB-ONS GIVE AN AGED LOOK AND HELP COORDINATE ITEMS ON A LAYOUT.

Couldn't Bee Any Cuter

• CREATE BACKGROUND BY ADHERING TRIMMED PATTERNED PAPER TO PURPLE PATTERNED PAPER • MAT PHOTOS WITH PURPLE PAPER AND ADHERE TO BACKGROUND • CREATE TITLE BY ATTACHING STICKERS TO SQUARE PIECES OF PURPLE PAPER • PRINT JOURNALING ON VELLUM AND MAT WITH PURPLE PAPER • MAT PURPLE CHECKED BORDER STICKER WITH PURPLE PAPER AND ADHERE TO TOP AND BOTTOM OF LAYOUT • EMBELLISH WITH BUMBLE BEE STICKERS (ATTACH TO SHEET PROTECTOR MATERIAL AND CUT OUT TO TAKE AWAY THE STICK) AND ADHERE TO LAYOUT WITH POP DOTS • SUPPLIES - PATTERNED PAPER: LEISURE ARTS; STICKERS: LEISURE ARTS

"Couldn't BEE any Cuter"

Darling Paul Charles on his first birthday, June 14th, 2003. He is such a happy and loveable little boy! His sweetness is emulated in his countenance of these photographs. Paul Charles is wearing his handsome Christening tuxedo.

P A U L

Designer: Sheila Hansen

Never underestimate the value of a little

moments

Moment

• CREATE BACKGROUND BY ADHERING PATTERNED PAPER, CHALKED PAPER AND GINGHAM RIBBON TO BROWN CARDSTOCK • PRINT TITLE ON PATTERNED PAPER AND ADHERE TO BACKGROUND • ATTACH LARGE PHOTO TO LAYOUT WITH PHOTO CORNERS • ADHERE PATTERNED PAPER, WATCH CUT OUT, SMALL PHOTO, GINGHAM RIBBON AND PEWTER LETTERS TO TAG • CREATE SMALL TAG BY TYING A CIRCLE TAG, HEART TAG AND SILVER TOGGLE TOGETHER WITH RIBBON • ADHERE TAGS TO LAYOUT • HANDWRITE AGE ON SQUARE METAL RIMMED TAG AND STRING WITH GINGHAM RIBBON • EMBELLISH LAYOUT WITH HEART CLIPS • SUPPLIES: PATTERNED PAPER: DMD COLLAGE PAPER, KAREN FOSTER; CARDSTOCK: BAZZILL

SPECIAL TIPS:

1. MINI GLUE DOTS HELP KEEP HANGING ITEMS IN PLACE.
2. CHALK PAPERS TO HELP THEM COORDINATE.

16

IT'S ALL ABOUT

DoubleTrouble

The twins each had their own 8" birthday cake. The party was held at Red Morten Park. Parents, Cousins, Aunts, Uncles, Grandparents, Great Grandparents, and Godparents attended.

June 14th 2003

Jiulia

Paul Charles

Designer: Sheila Hansen

FIRST BIRTHDAY

• CREATE BACKGROUND BY ADHERING TRIMMED GREEN PATTERNED PAPER TO YELLOW CARDSTOCK • MAT PHOTOS WITH COLORED PAPER AND ADHERE TO BACKGROUND • CREATE TITLE BY ATTACHING LETTER STICKERS TO SQUARE PIECES OF YELLOW PAPER • ADHERE TITLE TO BACKGROUND OVERLAPPING THE LETTERS • PRINT JOURNALING ON VELLUM AND ATTACH TO LAYOUT WITH GOLD MINI BRADS • CREATE BORDER AT BOTTOM BY ATTACHING STICKERS TO TWO STRIPS OF YELLOW PAPER •

SUPPLIES – PATTERNED PAPER: LEISURE ARTS; STICKERS: LEISURE ARTS

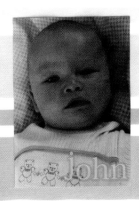

john

emily

Designer: Lynette Anderson

twice the fun

twice as nice

double the tears

seeing double

SEEING DOUBLE

- BEGIN WITH PATTERNED CARDSTOCK FOR BACKGROUND •
ADHERE PHOTOS TO BACKGROUND • ATTACH LETTER STICKERS
TO BACKGROUND AND PHOTOS FOR JOURNALING AND NAMES •
SUPPLIES – PAPER: SEI

TWINS

- CREATE BACKGROUND BY ADHERING TRIMMED
PATTERNED PAPER TO BLUE CARDSTOCK • MAT PHO-
TOS WITH PURPLE, SAGE AND WHITE CARDSTOCKS •
CREATE TITLE BY ADHERING GREEN ALPHABET
STICKERS TO MATTED CARDSTOCK SQUARES • CUT
OUT SMALL TAGS TO MAT CHARMS • ATTACH BOY
AND GIRL CHARMS WITH THREAD • EMBELLISH LAY-
OUT WITH THREADS •
SUPPLIES – PATTERNED PAPER: LEISURE ARTS; STICKERS:
LEISURE ARTS; METAL EMBELLISHMENTS:
TWOTWINKLES.COM; FIBER: TWOTWINKLES.COM

IT'S ALL ABOUT Smiles

13 months old

ALINA

CHERISH-verb
1. To have the highest regard for;
2. To recognize the worth, quality, importance, etc., of.
Syns: prize, treasure.-Idiom hold dear. Appreciate.

Designer: Anna Estrada Darvian

SPECIAL TIPS:
CONVERT PHOTOS TO SEPIA TONES TO GIVE VARIETY TO A PAGE.

ALINA

• CREATE BACKGROUND BY ADHERING PATTERNED PAPER, GREEN CORRUGATED CARDBOARD AND RIBBON TO TAN CARDSTOCK • MAT LARGE PHOTO WITH CARDSTOCK AND ADHERE TO BACKGROUND • MAT SMALLER PHOTOS WITH CARDBOARD AND ATTACH TO BACKGROUND WITH CHIFFON RIBBON AND BUTTON • CREATE TITLE WITH LETTER STICKERS • PRINT JOURNALING ONTO CARDSTOCK, TEAR AND INK EDGES AND ADHERE TO LAYOUT • HANDWRITE AGE • CREATE TAG BY CUTTING OUT PATTERNED PAPER AND ADHERING TO BACKGROUND • ADHERE TITLE TO LAYOUT OVERLAPPING TAG • EMBELLISH LAYOUT WITH RIBBON AND CHARM •
SUPPLIES – PATTERNED PAPER: 7 GYPSIES; LETTER STICKERS: NOSTALGIQUE, REBECCA SOWER; STAMP: ECLECTIC OMNIBUS; HEART CHARM: EMBELLISH IT

SMILE

- BEGIN WITH RED CARDSTOCK FOR BACK-GROUND • MAT PHOTOS TOGETHER WITH CARDSTOCK • CREATE TITLE WITH STICKERS AND METAL-RIMMED TAGS • FILL TAGS WITH DIE CUTS • EMBELLISH LAYOUT WITH PAPER SHAPES AND STICKERS •

SUPPLIES – CARDSTOCK: BAZZILL, SEI; STICKERS: SNIP IT'S, BRYCE & MADELINE, REBECCA SOWER; METAL TAGS: MAKING MEMORIES

SPECIAL TIPS:
MOUNTING SIMILAR PHOTOS TOGETHER ADDS IMPACT AND FOCUS.

Designer: Peggy Manrique

SPECIAL TIPS:
1. CHALK THE EDGES OF TORN PAPER TO GIVE AN ANTIQUED OR BURNT LOOK.
2. JOURNALING CAN SIMPLY BE WORDS DESCRIBING A PERSON. CHOOSE FONTS THAT FIT THE WORD YOU ARE USING.
3. TEXTURE AND DARK COLORS HELP CONTRAST PHOTOS.

3 MONTHS

- CREATE BACKGROUND BY ADHERING MESH AND AGED PAPER TO BROWN CARDSTOCK • ATTACH PHOTO TO BACKGROUND WITH METALLIC RUB-ON PHOTO CORNERS • ATTACH ALPHABET BLOCKS WITH SMALL SILVER BRADS TO CREATE TITLE • PRINT JOURNALING TEXT ONTO CARDSTOCK • TEAR AND CHALK EDGES OF JOURNALING PAGE • EMBELLISH WITH FRAME AND TOOTHPICKS TO CREATE TRAIN TRACKS • TIE GINGHAM RIBBON LIKE A PACKAGE AND ADHERE TO LAYOUT •

SUPPLIES – PATTERNED PAPER: LEGACY COLLAGE, CHATTERBOX, PATCHWORK PAPER; MESH: MAGIC MESH; LETTER BOXES: MY MIND'S EYE, THIS & THAT; BOOKPLATE: MAKING MEMORIES: PHOTO CORNERS: PIONEER; STICKERS: BO BUNNY; FONTS: DEAR JOE, BLACK BOYS ON MOPEDS, GILLIGANS ISLAND, FLOWERCHILD, LOV LETTERS, TYPEWRITER, FREESTYLE SCRIPT

Designer: Jan Cousins

My Favorite Photo

• CREATE BACKGROUND BY INKING EDGE OF WHITE CANVAS PHOTO PAPER • PRINT PHOTO ONTO CANVAS PAPER AND TEAR EDGES • ARRANGE ABSTRACT ART IMAGES IN TWO DIFFERENT SIZES ON THE COMPUTER • ADD TITLE TO LAYOUT ON COMPUTER • PRINT BLOCKS AND TITLE ONTO TRANSPARENCY • ADHERE TRANSPARENCY TO CANVAS • WRAP FIBER AROUND PHOTO • ADHERE POEM STONE TO HEART CONCH AND ADHERE TO PHOTO • ATTACH RUB-ON LETTERS FOR NAME AND DATE • ATTACH BLACK PHOTO CORNERS TO EDGE OF LAYOUT TO KEEP TRANSPARENCY ATTACHED TO CANVAS •
SUPPLIES — POEM STONE: SONNETS; FIBER: FIBERS BY THE YARD; RUB-ON LETTERS: STAPLES; FONT: CARPENTER

My First Bunny

• BEGIN WITH BLUE CARDSTOCK FOR BACKGROUND • TRIPLE MAT PHOTO AND ATTACH TO BACKGROUND WITH BLUE BRADS • PRINT JOURNALING ONTO CARDSTOCK AND DOUBLE MAT • HANDWRITE MESSAGE ON JOURNALING • ATTACH JOURNAL BLOCK WITH BLUE BRADS • USE TEMPLATE TO CUT OUT HEARTS • ADHERE HEARTS TO CARDSTOCK, DOUBLE MAT AND ADHERE TO LAYOUT •
SUPPLIES - CARDSTOCK: BAZZILL; BRADS: DOODLEBUG; HEARTS: QUICKUTS

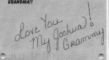

MY FIRST BUNNY

IN APRIL OF 2003, WE ALL WENT BACK TO OMAHA TO MEMORIALIZE THE MEMORY OF GREAT GRANDMA ROSE WHO HAD RECENTLY PASSED FROM OUR LIVES. ALL OF HER KIDS AND GRANDKIDS WERE THERE FOR THE SOLEMN EVENT. WE ALL MET ON THE LAST DAY AT THE OMAHA AIRPORT TO SAY OUR GOOD-BYES. THERE WAS GREAT AUNT BEV AND HER DAUGHTER LORI, AND LORI'S KIDS LEXI AND MOLLY, GREAT AUNT BARB AND GREAT UNCLE DICK AND THEIR KIDS, MICHELLE AND WENDY, GRANDMA AND GRANDPA NORTHUP, MY PARENTS SHAWN AND SARAH, AND MY AUNTIE MEAGHAN. GRANDMA MARIDAWN HAD BOUGHT ME MY FIRST BUNNY RABBIT, AND SURPRISED ME WITH THE GIFT AS I SAT ON GRANDPA FRANK'S LAP. AS YOU CAN SEE, I WAS OVERJOYED. THANKS GRANDMA!!

Love You
My Joshua!
Grammy

Hearts Filled With Love

- CREATE BACKGROUND BY ADHERING CUT PATTERNED PAPERS AND COLORED CARDSTOCKS TOGETHER IN STRIPED PATTERN • MAT PHOTO AND PRINTED JOURNALING BLOCK WITH CARDSTOCK • FRAME WITH CHIFFON RIBBON AND ATTACH WITH BRADS • RUN CHIFFON RIBBONS ACROSS LAYOUT AND ATTACH WITH BRADS •
SUPPLIES – PATTERNED PAPER: ANNA GRIFFIN; BRADS: DOODLEBUG

Babies bits of stardust blown from heaven to fill our hearts with hope and Love

Designer: MaryDawn Meyer

Mad

- CREATE BACKGROUND BY ADHERING STRIPED VELLUM, CIRCLE PATTERNED PAPER AND DARK BLUE PAPER TO GREEN CARDSTOCK • ADHERE PHOTO TO BACKGROUND • PRINT TITLE AND JOURNALING ONTO A COORDINATING SOLID PAPER AND ADHERE TO BACKGROUND • ADHERE TWO MATCHING FIBERS ACROSS LAYOUT • PLACE RUB-ON CIRCLES AND LETTER STICKERS ONTO EACH TAG • HANG VELLUM TAGS FROM FIBERS •
SUPPLIES – PATTERNED PAPER: CHATTERBOX, AMERICAN CRAFTS, MAKING MEMORIES; TAGWEAR: CREATIVE IMAGINATIONS; VELLUM TAG: MAKING MEMORIES; STICKERS: DAVID WALKER; FIBER: ADORNMENTS; FONT: YOU ARE WHAT YOU EAT

may 03   Jerry

mad

i just have to laugh sometimes when i see you trying to get mad. you are such a light-hearted and happy boy, that i don't think you even know how to really get mad. i snapped this photo at a moment when you didn't want to be photographed, and look at your face! what's funny is that one second later when i put the camera away, you were grinning from ear to ear again. my little mad boy!

IT'S ALL ABOUT

Seeing The World Through A
Childs Eyes

Designer: Jan Cousins

EXTREME CONCENTRATION

• CREATE BACKGROUND BY PRINTING PATTERNED PAPER USING VARIOUS FONTS FOR ONE WORD AND ADHERING IT TO BLACK CARDSTOCK • ADHERE THREE PHOTOS • ADHERE GINGHAM RIBBON ALONG THE BOTTOM OF THE PHOTOS • ATTACH GREEN STICKERS AND BRADWEAR LETTERS TO METAL-RIMMED TAGS • ATTACH TO BACKGROUND WITH SILVER EYELETS • RUB GREEN BRADWEAR ONTO BRADS • PRINT ONE 'CONCENTRATION' WORD IN GREEN • CUT OUT WORD AND PLACE ON PAGE PEBBLE • ADHERE TO LAYOUT WITH POP-DOT •

SUPPLIES – STICKERS: DOODLEBUG, CREATIVE IMAGINATIONS; EYELETS: MAKING MEMORIES; TAGS: MAKING MEMORIES; PAGE PEBBLE: MAKING MEMORIES

23

Feeding Ducks

• BEGIN WITH DARK GREEN CARDSTOCK FOR BACKGROUND • DOUBLE MAT THREE PHOTOS AND ADHERE TO BACKGROUND • MAT SIX PHOTOS TOGETHER AND ADHERE TO LIGHT GREEN CARDSTOCK • ADHERE MATTED PHOTOS TO BACKGROUND • CREATE TITLE BLOCK FROM RECTANGLE OF CARDSTOCK FRAMED ON TOP AND BOTTOM WITH STRIPS OF LIGHTER CARDSTOCK • REVERSE PRINT TITLE ON CARDSTOCK AND CUT OUT • CUT DUCKS FROM SCRAP PAPER AND ATTACH WITH BLACK BRADS FOR EYES • PRINT JOURNALING ONTO CARDSTOCK AND DOUBLE MAT • ADHERE TITLE AND JOURNALING TO BACKGROUND •
SUPPLIES - CARDSTOCK: BAZZILL

The World

• BEGIN WITH MAP PATTERNED PAPER FOR BACKGROUND • MAT PHOTOS • PRINT TITLE ONTO A TRANSPARENCY • FINISH TITLE WITH LETTER STICKERS • ADHERE TRANSPARENCY WITH CLEAR DOUBLE-SIDED TAPE • EMBELLISH WITH BOTTLE AND SHIP WHEEL •
SUPPLIES – PATTERNED PAPER: SONNETS; STICKERS: SONNETS; BOTTLE: JOLEE'S BOUTIQUE; SHIPS WHEEL: DRESS IT UP; FONT: TWO PEAS IN A BUCKET DREAMS

Hopes and Dreams

Dear child. I will care for you, protect you – until you are grown. And then I will let you fly free. But, loving you? That is for always.
~ *Charlotte Gray*

Designer: Jennifer Bourgeault

DEAR CHILD
• CREATE BACKGROUND BY PRINTING JOURNALING DIRECTLY ONTO TAN PAPER •
ADHERE TWO TORN COORDINATING PAPERS TO JOURNALING PAPER AND THEN
ADHERE TO BLACK CARDSTOCK • DEVELOP PHOTO IN SEPIA • ATTACH PHOTO TO
BACKGROUND WITH A STICKER FRAME • EMBELLISH WITH CIRCLE STICKERS •
SUPPLIES – PATTERNED PAPER: CHATTERBOX, ARTISTIC SCRAPPER; CARDSTOCK: BAZZILL;
FRAME: MY MIND'S EYE; BUTTONS: MY MIND'S EYE

Transparencies/Vellum

TRANSPARENCIES ARE A GREAT MEDIUM FOR TITLES, JOURNALING, GRAPHICS AND EVEN PHOTOS, AND ARE SO EASY TO USE. A TRANSPARENCY CAN GIVE ANY LOOK YOU ARE TRYING TO CREATE FROM OLD FASHIONED TO SHABBY CHIC. THE KEY TO CREATING THE PERFECT LOOK IS IN THE FONT AND BACKGROUND SELECTION. TO MAKE A TRANSPARENCY, JUST MEASURE WHERE THE TITLE OR JOURNALING SHOULD BE ON THE LAYOUT, PRINT OR HANDWRITE ONTO THE TRANSPARENCY AND ATTACH IT TO THE LAYOUT. YOU CAN EITHER ATTACH PIECES OF THE TRANSPARENCY TO THE LAYOUT OR THE ENTIRE TRANSPARENCY AS AN OVERLAY. YOU CAN ALSO ADD VARIETY TO YOUR TRANSPARENCIES BY PRINTING GRAPHICS AND PHOTOS, DRAWING WITH MARKERS AND BY PRINTING TEXT IN COLOR. PRINTING YOUR PHOTOS ONTO A TRANSPARENCY GIVES THEM A GREAT TRANSLUCENT QUALITY.

VELLUM IS ALSO A WONDERFUL CHOICE FOR OVERLAYS, TITLES, JOURNALING AND QUOTES. VELLUM COMES IN MANY DIFFERENT WEIGHTS, COLORS, DESIGNS AND TEXTURES. DON'T BE AFRAID TO PLAY AROUND WITH THE DIFFERENT OPTIONS TO SEE WHICH YOU LIKE BEST. MOST VELLUM WILL WORK FINE WITH AN INK-JET PRINTER BUT DOES EVEN BETTER WITH A LASER PRINTER.

VELLUM IS AN EXCELLENT MATERIAL FOR REPRESENTING WATER. CHOOSE WATER COLORED VELLUM, RIP THE EDGES AND LAYER WITH THE SAME COLOR OR COORDINATING COLORS. VELLUM'S TRANSLUCENT QUALITY ALSO GIVES AN ETHEREAL AND PURE LOOK TO THE SOFT AND HEAVENLY QUALITIES OF A NEWBORN BABE, CHILD AND BRIDE.

THE BEST GLUE TO USE IN ADHERING TRANSPARENCIES AND VELLUM TO A LAYOUT IS NONE AT ALL. TRY ATTACHING THEM WITH BRADS, EYELETS, STITCHES, NAIL HEADS, FIBERS, OR EVEN WEDGING AN EDGE UNDER ANOTHER ELEMENT ON A PAGE WITH A DROP OF GLUE. VELLUM TAPE CAN BE USED BUT USUALLY SHOWS THROUGH THE VELLUM. YOU CAN USE A XYRON MACHINE TO ADHERE TRANSPARENCIES AND VELLUM TO A LAYOUT, BUT BE AWARE THAT IT DOES CHANGE THE LOOK OF THE MEDIUM.

Designer: Jan Comarino

Lead, Guide, Walk

• CREATE BACKGROUND BY ADHERING PATTERNED PAPER WITH TORN AND CURLED EDGES TO TEXTURED SANDPAPER • SAND AND INK PAPER WITH SEPIA INK
• MAT PHOTOS WITH CARDSTOCK AND INK EDGES • ADHERE TORN VELLUM TO SOME PHOTOS WITH SCRAPPERS SPRAY • PUNCH FOCAL IMAGE FROM ONE
PHOTO WITH SQUARE PUNCH • MAT WITH CARDSTOCK AND PARCHMENT PAPER AND RE-ATTACH TO PHOTO WITH POP DOTS • INK AND ADHERE LETTER
STICKERS FOR TITLE • PRINT POEM ONTO TRANSPARENCY AND ADHERE OVER PHOTO OF FOOTPRINTS • EMBELLISH LAYOUT WITH SILVER FOOTPRINTS •
SUPPLIES – PATTERNED PAPER: CLUB SCRAPS, REBECCA SOWERS; FIBER: FIBERS BY THE YARD; FEET EYELETS: NAME-TRACES; TITLE: FOOFALA; FONTS: CK FLOURISH,
TWO PEAS IN A BUCKET BEACHBALL

Child of God

• CREATE BACKGROUND BY ADHERING COLORED PAPERS TO WHITE
CARDSTOCK • ADHERE PHOTOS TO BACKGROUND • ADHERE JOUR-
NALING TRANSPARENCY OVER LAYOUT • EMBELLISH WITH METAL
CHARMS, EYELETS, FLOSS AND METAL LETTERS •
SUPPLIES - PATTERNED PAPER: SEI; OVERLAY: ARTISTIC IMPRESSIONS

The Clean-Up

Designer: Sam Cousins

my dirty little valentine

My Dirty Little Valentine
• BEGIN WITH BLUE CARDSTOCK FOR BACKGROUND • PRINT PHOTO IN PANORAMIC SETTING •
ATTACH PHOTO TO BACKGROUND WITH PHOTO CORNERS • FRAME SMALL PHOTOS WITH
METAL FRAMES • ATTACH LETTER STICKERS FOR TITLE • MAT BORDER STICKER WITH TORN
WHITE CARDSTOCK •
Supplies – Stickers: Sonnets; Photo Corners: Making Memories; Frames: Making Memories

27

LET ME PLAY IN THE SUNSHINE; LET ME SING FOR JOY; LET ME GROW IN THE LIGHT; LET ME SPLASH IN THE RAIN, AND REMEMBER THE DAYS OF CHILDHOOD FOREVER.

ten little
fingers
&
ten little
toes

Sweet Dreams

LOOK

out

world,

here I

come

A sweet, new

blossom of Humanity,

Fresh fallen from

God's own home

—Gerald Massey,

There is no

birth & death,

save to enjoy

the interval.

—George Santayana

LET ME PLAY IN THE

SUNSHINE; LET ME SING

FOR JOY; LET ME GROW

IN THE LIGHT; LET ME

SPLASH IN THE RAIN,

AND REMEMBER THE

DAYS OF CHILDHOOD

FOREVER.

ten little

fingers

&

ten little

toes

Sweet Dreams

LOOK

out

world,

here I

come

A sweet, new

blossom of Humanity,

Fresh fallen from

God's own home

to flower on earth.

—Gerald Massey,
Wooed and Won

There is no

cure for

birth & death

save to enjoy

the interval.

—George Santayana

MOMS HOLD
LITTLE HANDS
NOW—HEARTS
FOREVER.

HUGS
&
KISSES

PRECIOUS
MEMORIES

Cute as a bug

mom & me

bundle of joy

Hugs & Kisses

MOMS HOLD
LITTLE HANDS
NOW—HEARTS
FOREVER.

PRECIOUS
MEMORIES

mom & me

Cute as can be

bundle of joy

I only have "FRIES" for you!!!

My Little Fry Guy!!!
I don't like giving you
french fries, because
I don't think they are
healthy. But they are
your new FAVORITE Food!!!
You don't like Ketchup,
like them 'naked' at
daddy cole it!!

I ONLY HAVE FRIES FOR YOU

• CREATE BACKGROUND BY ADHERING YELLOW CARDSTOCK TO RED CARDSTOCK • PRINT TITLE ONTO TRANS-PARENCY AND ADHERE WITH GLUE DOTS • PRINT JOURNALING ONTO WHITE CARDSTOCK AND MAT WITH BLUE CARDSTOCK • ATTACH JOURNALING WITH EYELETS • MAT ONE PHOTO • ADHERE ALL PHOTOS TO BACKGROUND • ADHERE A CLEAN McDonald's© FRY BAG • CREATE FRY SHAPES BY CUTTING YELLOW PAPER INTO STRIPS AND RUNNING THEM THROUGH A CRIMPER • SHADE FRIES WITH ORANGE CHALK • ADHERE INSIDE BAG AND RANDOM-LY THROUGHOUT LAYOUT •

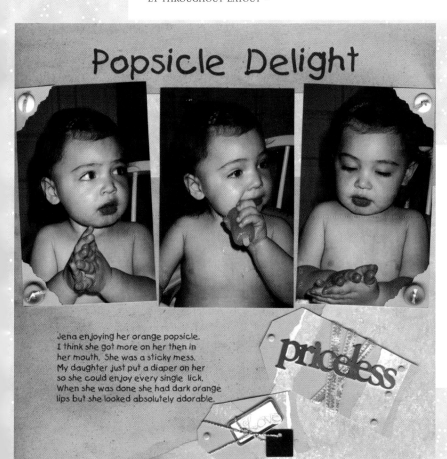

Popsicle Delight

Jena enjoying her orange popsicle.
I think she got more on her then in
her mouth. She was a sticky mess.
My daughter just put a diaper on her
so she could enjoy every single lick.
When she was done she had dark orange
lips but she looked absolutely adorable.

priceless

POPSICLE DELIGHT

• CREATE BACKGROUND BY ADHERING TWO TORN PIECES OF COMPLIMENTARY PAPER TO TEXTURED CARDSTOCK • ADHERE PHOTOS TO BACKGROUND • ATTACH STICKERS FOR TITLE • PRINT JOURNALING DIRECTLY ONTO BACKGROUND • CREATE TAGS WITH BACKGROUND PAPERS • EMBELLISH TAGS WITH TORN EDGES, METAL WORDS AND MINI BRADS • EMBELLISH PHOTOS WITH PHOTO CORNERS AND BUTTONS •
SUPPLIES – PATTERNED PAPER: KAREN FOSTER; METAL WORDS: MAKING MEMORIES; BRADS: GOOSE BARN; BUTTONS: MAKING MEMORIES; METAL SQUARE AND TAG: MAKING MEMORIES; STICKERS: K&CO.; FONT: FIRST GRADER

Holiday Fun

EASTER 2003

• CREATE BACKGROUND BY CUTTING A COORDINATING PAPER INTO EQUAL-SIZED RECTANGLES AND ADHERING THEM EQUALL[Y] SPACED TO PURPLE CARDSTOCK • CROP PHOTOS TO FIT WITHIN RECTANGLES • MAT SOME PHOTOS • CREATE TITLE IN ONE REC-TANGLE WITH STICKERS • PRINT CONTENTS OF EASTER BASKET ON VELLUM FOR JOURNALING • ATTACH JOURNALING ATOP AN EASTER BASKET PHOTO WITH STRIP STICKER ALLOWING VELLU[M] TO LIFT TO REVEAL PHOTO • FILL REMAINING BLOCKS WITH EMBELLISHMENTS • CREATE PURSE FREEHAND, ADHERE YELLO[W] FIBER FOR HANDLE AND MAKE BOW FROM LEFTOVER STICKERS • ATTACH PURSE TO BACKGROUND WITH POP-DOT • HAND STITC[H] GREEN FIBERS ACROSS PAGE WITH RANDOM CROSS-STITCHES •
SUPPLIES – PATTERNED PAPER: DOODLEBUG; CARDSTOCK: BAZZILL; STICKERS: SNIP IT'S, DAVID WALKER, SONNETS

SPECIAL TIPS:

1. THE STITCHING AND PURSE GIVE THE PAGE A HOME-MADE FEEL. THIS IS ESPECIALLY NICE FOR HOLIDAYS.
2. RANDOMLY SPACING PHOTOS KEEPS YOUR EYE MOVING ACROSS AND DOWN THE PAGE.
3. USING A VELLUM OVERLAY ALLOWS FOR JOURNALING WITHOUT DISTRACTING VIEWERS FROM THE PICTURES.
4. USING SIMPLE AND FUN TEXT CAN BE JUST AS MEMO-RABLE AS DESCRIBING THE ACTUAL EVENT.

MY FUNNY BUNNY

• CREATE BACKGROUND BY CHALKING PINK AND GREEN STRIPED PAPER AND TEARING A RANDOM HOLE OUT OF THE CENTER OF THE PAPER • CRUMPLE AND SAND MATCHING CARDSTOCK AND ADHERE TO THE BACK OF PATTERNED PAPER UNDER TORN HOLE • MAT ONE PHOTO WITH WHITE CARDSTOCK • TEAR AND CHALK EDGES OF OTHER PHOTO • CREATE TITLE BY STRINGING LETTER BEADS ON FIBER AND ATTACHING TO LAYOUT WITH BRADS • ATTACH STICKERS TO FINISH TITLE • CREATE TAG FROM WHITE CARDSTOCK AND STRIPED PAPER • EMBELLISH TAG WITH RIBBON AND STICKERS • ADHERE FIBER ACROSS LAYOUT • ATTACH GRASS STICKER, EGGS AND TAG TO LAYOUT • EMBELLISH WITH BLACK PHOTO CORNERS AND ROUND SILVER EYELETS • OUTLINE LAYOUT AND TAG WITH PEN •
SUPPLIES – PATTERNED PAPER: LEISURE ARTS; LETTER BEADS: TARGET; FIBER: FIBERS BY THE YARD; STICKERS: JOLEE'S, LEISURE ARTS

SPECIAL TIPS:

1. TEAR PHOTOS FOR A DIF-FERENT LOOK.
2. ATTACH BRADS AND EYE-LETS TO PHOTOS FOR ACCENTS.

Clowning Around

- CREATE BACKGROUND BY ADHERING TRIMMED LINE PATTERNED PAPER TO CIRCLE PATTERNED PAPER • ADHERE CUT STRIP OF GREEN CARDSTOCK AND TENT TOP OF CIRCLE PATTERNED PAPER TO BACKGROUND • MAT PHOTO WITH PATTERNED PAPERS AND CARD-STOCKS • REVERSE PRINT TITLE AND CUT OUT • MAT WITH COLORED CARDSTOCK, CUT OUT AND ADHERE TO BACKGROUND • ADHERE TAG WITH HANDWRITTEN JOURNALING • ADHERE CLOWN EMBELLISHMENT TO LAYOUT •

Designer: Eleanor Finnie

Santa Baby

- BEGIN WITH RED CARDSTOCK FOR BACKGROUND • MAT PHOTO ON RED AND WHITE CARDSTOCK • MAT THREE PHOTOS IN A STRIP ON WHITE CARD-STOCK • ADHERE PHOTO STRIP TO BOTTOM OF BACKGROUND AND OTHER PHOTO IN UPPER RIGHT CORNER • PRINT TITLE AND JOURNALING ON WHITE CARDSTOCK • USE "NIGHT BEFORE CHRISTMAS" POEM AS BASIS FOR JOURNALING • CUT, MAT WITH RED AND WHITE CARDSTOCK AND ADHERE TO BACKGROUND • EMBELLISH LAYOUT WITH FIBERS TO MIMIC BOA IN PHOTO • SUPPLIES – FIBER: FIBERS BY THE YARD; FONT: BRADLEY HAND

Designer: Jan Cousins

Peek-A-Boo

- CREATE BACKGROUND BY ADHERING A TORN PIECE OF PATTERNED PAPER TO A COORDINATING PATTERNED PAPER • ADHERE CUT CHEESECLOTH ACROSS LAYOUT • ADHERE MAIN PHOTO TO BACKGROUND • FRAME OTHER PHOTO AND ADHERE TO BACKGROUND • CREATE TITLE WITH VARYING STICKERS AND A HANDWRITTEN TRANSPARENCY FOR 'I See You' • PRINT JOURNALING ON PATTERNED PAPER AND TRANSPARENCY AND ADHERE TO LAYOUT • CREATE TAG WITH PATTERNED PAPER AND STICKERS • ATTACH WITH BRAD • THREAD BEADS ONTO WIRE AND ATTACH WITH BRAD • EMBELLISH CHEESECLOTH BY ATTACHING BEADS WITH DIAMOND GLAZE •

Supplies – Patterned Paper: NRN Designs; Stickers: NRN Designs, Mary Engelbreit, Rebecca Sower, Making Memories; Frame: NRN Designs; Tag: NRN Designs

Treasure

- BEGIN WITH BLUE CARDSTOCK FOR BACKGROUND • EMBELLISH PHOTO WITH TORN AND INKED CARDSTOCKS AND PATTERNED PAPER • MAT PHOTO AND INK EDGES • REVERSE PRINT TITLE AND CUT OUT • ADHERE MESH OVER TITLE • PRINT JOURNALING ON WHITE CARDSTOCK, INK EDGES AND MAT • USE A TEMPLATE TO ARRANGE PHOTO AND JOURNALING BLOCKS AND ADHERE TO BACKGROUND • CUT STRIP OF PATTERNED PAPER AND ADHERE EMBELLISHMENTS •

Supplies – Cardstock: Bazzill; Stickers: Jolee's Boutique; Mesh: Magic Mesh; Font: Saffron Too

Connor has always required a certain amount of gentleness, especially when he was brought into any new situation. People would have to spend a lot of time just being in the same room, then talking at a distance, then communicating close up, before they made an attempt at physical contact. Connor's sensitivity has only made me feel more important and I love providing Connor with the patience and understanding he needs.

Be gentle with all the world's treasures.

HOME GROWN

• CREATE BACKGROUND BY ADHERING BLACK, RED AND FAWN CARDSTOCKS AND PATTERNED PAPER IN A COLLAGE • DISTRESS BACKGROUND IN SMEARING FASHION WITH BLACK INK • MAT PHOTOS AND ADHERE TO BACKGROUND • CREATE TITLE BY MATTING METAL EYELET WORD WITH GINGHAM RIBBON AND STAMPING FAWN CARDSTOCK WITH BLOCK LETTER STAMPS • TEAR BLOCK LETTERS, CHALK EDGES AND ATTACH TO LAYOUT WITH RED EYELETS • CREATE BORDER BY ADHERING A KNOTTED GINGHAM RIBBON TO FAWN AND RED CARDSTOCKS AND STAMP DATE • EMBELLISH LAYOUT WITH TAN MESH, THREE PEWTER STAR EYELETS AND BUTTON •

SUPPLIES – PATTERNED PAPER: 7 GYPSIES; INK PAD: HERO ARTS; EYELETS: MAKING MEMORIES; DATE STAMP: MAKING MEMORIES; METAL EMBELLISHMENTS: MAKING MEMORIES; STAMP: HERO ARTS; CHALKS: STAMPIN' UP

Designer: Tammy Mellish

CLASS OF 2020

• CREATE BACKGROUND BY ADHERING RANDOMLY TORN PATTERNED PAPER TO CORRUGATED CARDBOARD • DISTRESS BACKGROUND WITH SEPIA INK PAD • MAT PHOTO WITH PIECE OF CARDBOARD AND ATTACH TO BACKGROUND WITH MINI METAL BRADS • CREATE NAME PORTION OF TITLE BY ATTACHING INKED LETTER STICKERS TO BACKGROUND • PRINT REST OF TITLE ONTO TRANSPARENCY AND ADHERE OVER CARDBOARD • MAT QUOTE STICKER WITH INKED CARDBOARD • EMBELLISH QUOTE WITH FIBER •

SUPPLIES – STICKERS: CLUB SCRAP JOURNEY KIT; FIBER: FIBERS BY THE YARD; FONT: BATIK

IT'S ALL ABOUT

Growing-Up

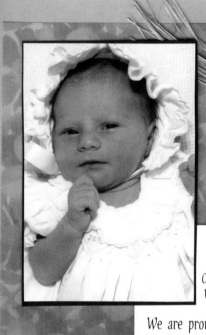

She's finally here, she finally arrived,
A beautiful baby has entered our lives.
Our family is thrilled, as you may have guessed,
We're very thankful that we've been so blessed.

We are proud to announce
the arrival of

Anna Marie

July 2, 2003
7 pounds, 5.8 ounces
20½ inches

Jennifer and Jamie Reardon
& Big Brother Cole

birth (burth) 1. the act of bringing a child into the world 2. bringing forth offspring 3. the beginning of anything   precious (presh´-es) 1. of great worth 2. beloved; cherished

Designer: Christi Fratini

ANNA MARIE

• CREATE BACKGROUND BY ADHERING FLOWER PATTERNED VELLUM TO YELLOW CARDSTOCK • MAT PHOTO WITH BLACK CARDSTOCK AND ADHERE TO BACKGROUND • ADHERE BABY ANNOUNCEMENT TO BACKGROUND • ADHERE PRE-MADE TAG TO BACKGROUND • EMBELLISH LAYOUT WITH CHALKED BIRTH DEFINITION STICKER AND RAFFIA •

SUPPLIES – VELLUM: WORLDWIN; CARDSTOCK: BAZZILL; TAGS: FRESH TAGS, REBECCA SOWER; STICKERS: MAKING MEMORIES; CHALK: CLOSE TO MY HEART

JOSH

- BEGIN WITH YELLOW CARDSTOCK FOR BACK-GROUND • DOUBLE MAT PHOTOS AND ADHERE TO BACKGROUND • CREATE TITLE CARD BY PRINTING DATE AND AGE ONTO WHITE CARD-STOCK • ATTACH LETTER STICKERS TO TITLE CARD WITH GREEN BRADS • PRINT JOURNALING ONTO CARDSTOCK, DOUBLE MAT AND ADHERE TO BACKGROUND • MAT METAL PLATE WITH TORN PAPER AND DOUBLE MAT WITH CARDSTOCK • ATTACH TO BACKGROUND WITH STAR BRADS • ADHERE GREEN VELLUM ENVELOPE TO BACK-GROUND AND INSERT TITLE CARD • EMBELLISH LAYOUT WITH ANIMAL STICKERS TO MATCH BABY'S BIB •

SUPPLIES — CARDSTOCK: NATIONAL CARDSTOCK; METAL ACCENT: MAKING MEMORIES; ENVELOPE: EK SUCCESS; STICKERS: EK SUCCESS; STAR BRADS: CREATIVE IMAGINATIONS; LETTER STICKERS: EK SUCCESS; GREEN EYELETS: DOODLEBUG

May 31, 2003
4 Months 3 weeks

CHERUB (cher'-eb) 1. a type of angel characterized as a chubby, rosy cheeked child with wings 2. a child with a sweet, innocent face

Designer: MaryDawn Mayer

2 MONTHS

- CREATE BACKGROUND BY ADHERING CURSIVE PATTERNED PAPER AND NATURAL COLORED CARDSTOCK TO FLOWER PATTERNED PAPER • ATTACH GINGHAM STICKER STRIP TO SEPARATE DIFFERENT PAPERS • MAT PHOTO WITH TORN MULBERRY PAPER AND ADHERE TO PAGE • TRIM PICTURE TO FIT METAL FRAME AND ADHERE WITH GLUE DOTS • ATTACH LETTER STICKERS FOR TITLE • PRINT JOURNALING ONTO VELLUM AND ADHERE TO LAYOUT • EMBELLISH LAYOUT WITH BABY SAFETY PINS AND PHOTO CORNERS •

SUPPLIES — PATTERNED PAPER: ANNA GRIFFIN, 7 GYPSIES; MULBERRY PAPER: BAZZILL; STICKERS: STICKOPOTAMUS, REBECCA SOWER; METAL FRAME: MAKING MEMORIES; BABY PINS: JOLEE'S BY YOU

SPECIAL TIPS:

WET MULBERRY PAPER BEFORE TEARING EDGES TO GIVE IT A SOFT, FLUFFY TEXTURE.

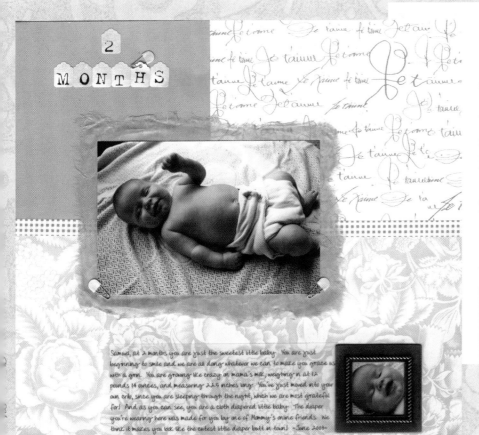

34

IT'S ALL ABOUT
Head, Shoulders, Knees And Toes

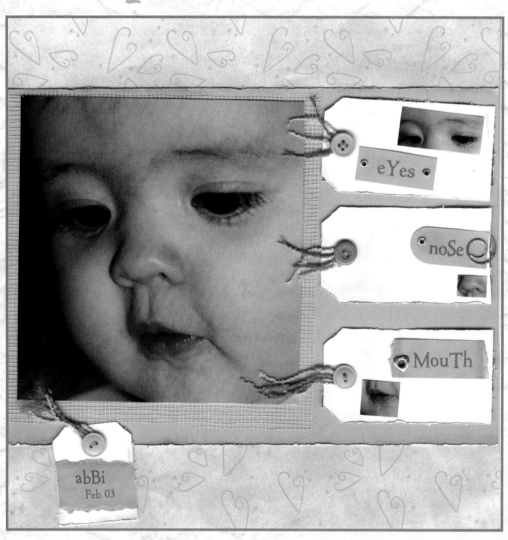

Designer: Jodi Sanford

(On layout: eYes, noSe, MouTh, abBi Feb 03)

ABBI FACE

- CREATE BACKGROUND BY ADHERING TORN PIECE OF CARDSTOCK WITH INKED EDGES TO PATTERNED PAPER • MAT ENLARGED PHOTO WITH MESH AND ADHERE TO BACKGROUND • CREATE WORD BLOCKS WITH CARDSTOCK AND STAMPS • PRINT JOURNALING ONTO VELLUM AND ADHERE TO LAYOUT • TEAR TAGS AND RUB WITH CHALKS • ATTACH WORD BLOCKS TO TAGS WITH EYELETS • CUT PORTIONS OF PHOTO AND ADHERE TO TAGS • ADHERE TAGS TO LAYOUT OVER JOURNALING VELLUM • EMBELLISH TAGS WITH BUTTONS, FIBERS AND CLIPS •

SUPPLIES – PATTERNED PAPER: PROVO CRAFT; MESH: MAGENTA'S

CHANGES IN YOU

• BEGIN WITH PATTERNED PAPER FOR BACK-
GROUND AND AGE WITH INK • DOUBLE MAT
PHOTOS AND ADHERE TO BACKGROUND •
PRINT TITLE ONTO CARDSTOCK AND ADHERE
TO BACKGROUND • PRINT JOURNALING ONTO
VELLUM, MAT WITH CARDSTOCK AND ADHERE
TO BACKGROUND • HEAT EMBOSS JOURNALING
WITH CLEAR EMBOSSING POWDER • EMBELLISH
LAYOUT WITH CHARM AND BRADS •
SUPPLIES – PATTERNED PAPER: DESIGN ORIGINALS;
BRADS: MAKING MEMORIES; LETTER STICKERS:
SHOTZ; SILVER CHARM: HOBBY LOBBY; FONT:
PROBLEM SECRETARY

SPECIAL TIPS:

USE BLACK AND WHITE PHOTO
PAPER WHEN DEVELOPING
BLACK AND WHITE FILM. IT
MAY BE MORE COSTLY, BUT
THE RESULTS ARE STRIKING.

Designer: Anna Estrada Davison

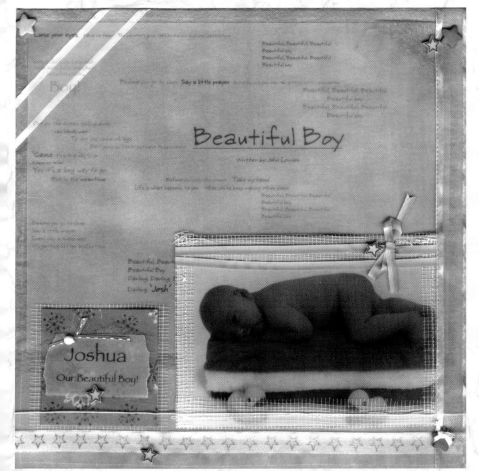

BEAUTIFUL BOY

• CREATE BACKGROUND BY ADHERING TORN
BLUE NETTING AND A SHEET OF VELLUM TO PAT-
TERNED PAPER • ATTACH MESH TO PHOTO WITH
STITCHING • PRINT LYRICS TO "BEAUTIFUL
BOY" BY JOHN LENNON ON WHITE VELLUM •
ARRANGE LYRICS THROUGHOUT THE PAGE AND
PRINT IN GRAY TONES • ADHERE VELLUM TO
LAYOUT • PRINT TITLE ONTO VELLUM AND MAT
WITH PATTERNED VELLUM, MATCHING PAPER
AND NETTING • EMBELLISH LAYOUT WITH RIB-
BON, NETTING, STARS AND BRADS •
SUPPLIES – VELLUM: DCWV, LEISURE ARTS;
BUTTONS: DRESS IT UP

IT'S ALL ABOUT

Babies
On The Move

Joshua

- CREATE BACKGROUND BY ADHERING STRIP OF LIGHT BLUE PATTERNED PAPER AND ZIPPER TO PATTERNED PAPER • MAT LARGE PHOTO AND STRIP OF SMALLER PHOTOS • SEW TOP EDGE OF LARGE PHOTO TO ATTACH TO BACKGROUND • REVERSE PRINT TITLE LETTERING AND CUT OUT • MAT LETTERS AND CUT OUT AGAIN • ATTACH PRINTED JOURNALING WITH BRADS • EMBELLISH WITH CHARM AND SILVER LETTERS •

Supplies – Cardstock: Bazzill; Patterned Paper: Bo Bunny; Zipper: Junkitz; Letter Stickers: Making Memories; Metal Charms: Leisure Arts; Title: Quickutz

CLIMB HIGH

• BEGIN WITH TEXTURED CARDSTOCK FOR
BACKGROUND • MAT AND ADHERE THREE
PHOTOS TO BACKGROUND • ADHERE CLIMB
HIGH QUOTE WITH BRASS EYELETS • STAMP
DATE • CUT TWIG FROM PAPER AND ADHERE
TO BOTTOM OF PHOTOS OVER PORTION OF
QUOTE • EMBELLISH LAYOUT WITH THREE
BRASS EYELETS •
SUPPLIES – PAPER: REBECCA SOWER; QUOTES:
MEMORIES COMPLETE; DATE STAMP: MAKING
MEMORIES

climb high,
climb far,
your goal
the sky
your aim
the star.

- Williams College Inscription

Summer 2003

Designer: Pam Canavan

7 Months

Li'l
Babe

LI'L BABE

• CREATE BACKGROUND BY ADHERING STRIPS OF CARDSTOCK AND PAT-
TERNED PAPER TO TAN CARDSTOCK • DOUBLE MAT PHOTOS AND
ADHERE TO BACKGROUND • ADHERE LETTER DIE CUTS FOR TITLE AND
JOURNALING • EMBELLISH LAYOUT WITH BASEBALL BRADS •
SUPPLIES – CARDSTOCK: BAZZILL; PATTERNED PAPER: DOODLEBUG; BUTTONS:
JESSE JAMES; TITLE: QUICKUTZ

It's All About

In Touch With Nature

Designer: Camille Jensen

GROW

• CREATE BACKGROUND BY ADHERING TORN AND EMBOSSED GREEN PATTERNED PAPER (EMBOSS BY STAMPING WITH A CLEAR EMBOSSING PAD AND HEAT EMBOSSING SEVERAL TIMES) TO PURPLE PATTERNED PAPER • ATTACH PICTURE TO BACKGROUND WITH PHOTO CORNERS • CREATE TITLE WITH LETTER STICKERS ON METAL-RIMMED TAGS • EMBOSS EACH TAG WITH DEEP EMBOSSING POWDER • LET TAGS COOL AND CRACK BY GENTLY BENDING TAG • ADHERE GREEN AND YELLOW RIBBON TO LAYOUT • ATTACH NAME TAG TO LAYOUT WITH RIBBON • ATTACH TITLE TO LAYOUT WITH BRADS • ADHERE LAMINATED DRY DAISY WITH SQUARE TAG TO LAYOUT •
Supplies – Patterned Paper: Leisure Arts; Deep Embossing: Suze Weinberg; Stickers: Leisure Arts; Tags: Avery

BUBBLE

• BEGIN WITH PATTERNED PAPER FOR BACKGROUND • ALTER ONE PICTURE TO SEPIA TONE • ADHERE PHOTOS TO BACKGROUND • PRINT TITLE ONTO PATTERNED PAPER • PRINT JOURNALING ON VELLUM • REPLACE CENTERS OF METAL TAGS WITH COLORED VELLUM • ADD SPARKLES TO MAKE TAGS LOOK LIKE BUBBLES • ADHERE TITLE, JOURNALING AND BUBBLES TO LAYOUT •
Supplies – Patterned Paper: Sonnets; Metal Tags: Making Memories

May your joys be as deep as the ocean and your sorrows as light as foam.

Designer: Sara Horton

Crystal Lacquer/Clear Embossing

CRYSTAL LACQUER IS A THICK LIQUID THAT DRIES TO FORM A RAISED SOLID. IT WILL DRAW ATTENTION TO WHATEVER IT IS APPLIED TO AND WILL MAGNIFY TEXT OR SHAPES UNDERNEATH IT. BE SURE TO SQUEEZE THE LIQUID ONTO YOUR LAYOUT CAREFULLY TO AVOID AIR BUBBLES. CRYSTAL LACQUER CAN BE USED AS A LACQUER AND AN ADHESIVE. IT IS A GREAT ADHESIVE FOR WATCH CRYSTALS AND OTHER CLEAR PRODUCTS. CRYSTAL LACQUER CAN BE PURCHASED IN A CLEAR OR PRE-COLORED FORM.

CLEAR EMBOSSING POWDER COMES IN TWO DIFFERENT FORMS: 1) REGULAR CLEAR EMBOSSING POWDER HAS A FINE TEXTURE AND CREATES A THIN GLASS-LIKE COATING; 2) THICK CLEAR EMBOSSING POWDER IS HEAT EMBOSSED IN SEVERAL LAYERS TO GIVE A VERY THICK CLEAR COATING.

TO EMBOSS, INK WITH PIGMENT INK, DUST AREA WITH EMBOSSING POWDER, SHAKE OFF EXCESS POWDER AND HEAT. IF USING THICK EMBOSSING POWDER IN A LARGE AREA, REPEAT THE EMBOSSING PROCESS SEVERAL TIMES OVER ONE SMALL AREA AT A TIME. WHEN FINISHED, LET COOL (PUT IN THE FREEZER FOR A MOMENT IF YOU ARE IN A HURRY). TO GET A CRACKLED OR AGED EFFECT GENTLY BEND EMBOSSED AREA BACK AND FORTH. ANY SCRAPBOOKING ELEMENT CAN BE CLEAR EMBOSSED FOR DIMENSION. ADD PAINT OR INK TO CLEAR EMBOSSING TO CHANGE THE LOOK OR COLOR OF AN ELEMENT.

DANDY LION SPRING

• BEGIN WITH GRAY CARDSTOCK FOR BACKGROUND • MAT PHOTOS WITH WHITE CARDSTOCK AND ADHERE TO BACKGROUND • PRINT TITLE ON CARDSTOCK, INK EDGES, MAT WITH DISTRESSED PAPER (CRUMPLE AND SAND PAPER WITH FINE GRAIN SAND PAPER) AND ATTACH TO BACK-GROUND WITH SILVER BRAD AND THREAD • PRINT JOURNALING AND INK EDGES • CREATE LARGE TAG FROM WHITE CARDSTOCK, PHOTO AND CRUMPLED PAPER • PLACE A SMALL AMOUNT OF FUN FLOCK IN A WATCH CRYSTAL AND GLUE TO THE TAG WITH DIAMOND GLAZE • SEW ELEMENTS TOGETHER FOR TAG • INK SMALL TAGS • EMBELLISH LAYOUT WITH PIECES OF CRUMPLED PAPER, THREAD, CHARMS, TAGS, SAFETY PINS, BRADS AND EYELETS •

SUPPLIES – CARDSTOCK: CLOSE TO MY HEART, PATCHWORK MEMORIES; BUTTERFLY NAIL HEADS: JEST CHARMING; BRADS: JEST CHARMING: EYELETS: JEST CHARMING; FIBERS: BROWN BAG FIBERS; TAGS: DMD; INK: CLEARSNAP; FUN FLOCK: STAMPIN' UP; WATCH CRYSTAL: TWO PEAS IN A BUCKET; FONT: TWO PEAS IN A BUCKET FLEA MARKET

SPECIAL TIPS:

1. TO MOUNT NAIL HEADS TO TAGS:
   A. PLACE TAGS ON A MOUSE PAD.
   B. PRESS NAIL HEADS INTO TAGS GENTLY. IF NECESSARY, REMOVE NAIL HEADS; USE A CRAFT KNIFE TO CREATE HOLES, THEN PUSH NAIL HEADS THROUGH.
   C. TURN TAG OVER AND USE THE END OF A PEN TO PRESS THE SPIKES TOWARD THE CENTER. MAKE SURE ALL PRONGS ARE COMPLETELY FLATTENED.
2. SAFETY PINS ARE AN INEXPENSIVE AND INTER-ESTING WAY TO HANG ELEMENTS FROM A SCRAPBOOK PAGE.

IT'S ALL ABOUT
Mother Nature

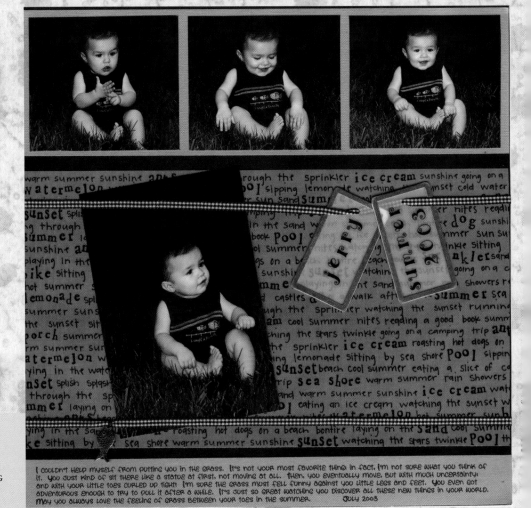

SUMMER 2003

- CREATE BACKGROUND BY ADHERING TRIMMED PRINTED VELLUM TO TEXTURED CARDSTOCK • ADHERE MAIN PHOTO TO BACKGROUND • MAT THREE SMALLER PHOTOS AND ADHERE TO BACKGROUND • ADHERE LETTERS TO VELLUM TAGS FOR TITLE • PRINT JOURNALING ONTO ORANGE CARDSTOCK AND ADHERE TO BOTTOM OF LAYOUT • RUN TWO PIECES OF GINGHAM RIBBON ACROSS LAYOUT • STRING VELLUM TAGS FROM TOP RIBBON • STRING SILVER FISH CHARM FROM BOTTOM RIBBON •

Supplies – Cardstock: Bazzill; Printed Vellum: Over the Moon; Letter Sticker: Provo Craft

SPECIAL TIPS:

1. TO PRINT JOURNALING 12" WIDE, SET THE PAPER SIZE TO LEGAL (8I/2X14) AND THE PAPER DIRECTION TO LANDSCAPE ON THE COMPUTER.
2. PULL ACCENTS FOR THE PAGE FROM THE PHOTOS (I.E. THE FISH CHARM ACCENT CAME FROM THE FISH ON THE LITTLE BOY'S SHIRT).
3. MOUNT SEVERAL SMALL PHOTOS CLOSE TOGETHER TO SHOW A SEQUENCE OF EVENTS.

True Beauty

- BEGIN WITH PURPLE CARDSTOCK FOR BACKGROUND • CUT 8x10 PHOTO INTO STRIPS ALONG TOP AND BOTTOM EDGE OF THE PHOTO • ADHERE TO BACKGROUND SPACING THE STRIPS TO REVEAL CARDSTOCK BACKGROUND • CUT OUT TITLE USING REVERSE LETTERING AND ADHERE TO BACKGROUND • PRINT JOURNALING ON GREEN CARDSTOCK AND ADHERE TO LAYOUT • ADHERE THIN STRIPS OF NAVY CARDSTOCK TO LAYOUT • INK EDGES WITH BROWN INK • EMBELLISH LAYOUT WITH FLOWERS •
Supplies – Cardstock: Bazzill; 3-D Stickers: Jolee's; Font: Brock Script, Two Peas in a Bucket Kathryn Brooks

Good Old Summertime

- CREATE BACKGROUND BY DECORATIVELY SEWING TRIMMED PATTERNED PAPER TO RED CARDSTOCK WITH A VINE STITCH • DOUBLE MAT PHOTO • PUNCH SMALL HOLES ALONG BOTTOM OF MAT EVERY 1/2" • ATTACH FIBERS AND GLASS BEADS TO MAT BY WEAVING LOOSELY • ADHERE MATTED PHOTO TO LAYOUT • USE Fortunaschwein FONT FOR TITLE • PRINT TITLE REVERSED ON GREEN PAPER AND CUT OUT • ADHERE TITLE TO BACKGROUND IN A CURVE • PRINT JOURNALING ON VELLUM AND FIT INSIDE SLIDE HOLDER THAT HAS BEEN COVERED WITH GOLD FABRIC • WRAP BOTTOM EDGE OF SLIDE HOLDER WITH FIBERS AND BEADS • ATTACH TWISTED FIBERS ACROSS LAYOUT AND ADHERE SLIDE HOLDER OVER FIBERS • EMBELLISH LAYOUT WITH SUN CHARM •
Supplies – Cardstock: Bazzill, Making Memories; Vellum: Paper Adventures; Fibers: Fibers By The Yard; Sun Charm: All the Extras; Gold Fabric: Hobby Lobby; Thread: Coats; Slide Holder: All the Extras; Glass Beads: All the Extras; Font: Fortunaschwein

Designer: Jason Stringfellow

Wherever You Go

- CREATE BACKGROUND BY ADHERING STICKER BORDERS TO THE TOP AND BOTTOM OF A SHEET OF PATTERNED CARDSTOCK • MAT PHOTOS WITH TAN CARDSTOCK AND INK THE EDGES • CREATE TITLE BY STAMPING AND ATTACHING STICKERS TO THE BACKGROUND • ATTACH VELLUM TO BACKGROUND WITH MINI SILVER BRADS •
Supplies – Patterned Paper: Club Scraps; Stamps: PSX; Letter Stickers: Stampendous, Making Memories

Sun, Sea & Sand

Designer: Tammy Gauck

FIRST TIME FEELING SAND

• CREATE BACKGROUND BY ADHERING TORN BLUE PAPER TO PLAID PAT-
TERNED PAPER • MAT TOP PHOTO AND TEAR BOTTOM EDGE • ADHERE
TORN AND EMBOSSED PIECE OF PAPER TO SAND PHOTO • EMBOSS EDGES
OF TORN PAPERS BEFORE ADHERING TO LAYOUT • ATTACH STICKER LET-
TERS FOR TITLE • STAMP CLOCK ON TITLE PAPER WITH WHITE INK •
HANDWRITE DATE ON VELLUM TAG AND ATTACH TO LAYOUT WITH
STARFISH CHARM AND FLOSS • FILL WATCH CRYSTAL WITH SAND AND
ADHERE TO TITLE • EMBELLISH WITH SHELLS, SAND, STARFISH AND
SAND DOLLAR •

SUPPLIES – PAPER: MAKING MEMORIES, ROBINS NEST; LETTER STICKERS:
SONNETS, STAMPIN' UP; TAG: MAKING MEMORIES; FLOSS: DMC; WATCH
CRYSTAL: SCRAPSAHOY.COM; STAMPS: INKADINKADOO

Chasing Seagulls

CHASING SEAGULLS

• BEGIN WITH TEXTURED CARDSTOCK FOR BACKGROUND • CROP PORTION OF PHOTO ON COMPUTER, PRINT OUT, TEAR EDGES AND ADHERE TO BACKGROUND • PRINT TITLE IN LANDSCAPE MODE ON WHITE CARDSTOCK • TEAR BOTTOM EDGE OF TITLE PAPER • APPLY LIQUID GLUE TO TORN EDGE AND SPRINKLE WITH GLITTER • ADHERE TO BACKGROUND • TYPE JOURNALING OVER PHOTO, PRINT OUT AND CUT INTO STRIPS • ATTACH JOURNALING STRIPS TO BACKGROUND WITH BRADS • CUT THREE PIECES OF FLOSS AND TIE A KNOT AT ONE END • ATTACH BLUE MOON BEADS, SAND DOLLAR AND MINI METAL FRAMED PHOTO TO ENDS OF FLOSS AND KNOT • EMBELLISH WITH SEASHELL DIE CUTS •
SUPPLIES – CARDSTOCK: BAZZILL; GLITTER: JONES TONES; FLOSS: DMC; BEADS: BLUE MOON; TAG: MAKING MEMORIES; DIECUT: JOLEE'S BOUTIQUE; FONT: CK BELLA

YOU AND ME BY THE SEA

• CREATE BACKGROUND BY ADHERING TORN STRIPS OF BLUE PAPER TO WHITE CARDSTOCK RESEMBLING WAVES OF THE SEA • MAT PHOTOS WITH CARDSTOCK AND ADHERE TO BACKGROUND • CREATE TITLE WITH RUB-ON LETTERS AND LETTER STAMPS • ADHERE DIE CUTS TO THE BACKGROUND • WRAP FIBER AROUND ENTIRE LAYOUT AND TIE OFF • EMBELLISH WITH POEMSTONE AND FLOWER SHAPES •
SUPPLIES – PATTERNED PAPER: LEISURE ARTS; DIECUTS: DELUXE CUTS; METAL FLOWERS: LEISURE ARTS; POEM STONES: SONNETS; TITLE: CREATIVE IMAGINATIONS; STAMPS: PSX; FIBERS: FIBER BY THE YARD

SPECIAL TIPS:

1. USE PRODUCTS FOR A PURPOSE OTHER THAN INTENDED. THE LITTLE FLOWER SHAPES ARE FROM A BABY CHARM KIT.
2. TEAR UP AND RE-PIECE A PAPER TO FIT YOUR NEEDS.

Designer: Pam Coulson

44

IT'S ALL ABOUT

Water Babies

WATER BOY

- CREATE BACKGROUND BY ADHERING DISTRESSED BLUE CARDSTOCK AND A STRIP OF DARK BLUE CARDSTOCK TO TEXTURED CARDSTOCK • DOUBLE MAT PHOTO WITH CARDSTOCK AND ADHERE TO BACKGROUND • REVERSE PRINT TITLE AND CUT OUT WITH EXACTO KNIFE • FINISH TITLE WITH DOMINO PIECES STAMPED WITH LETTERS • EMBELLISH WITH METALLIC RUB-ONS TO ADD DIMENSION TO THE DISTRESSED PAPER •

SUPPLIES – CARDSTOCK: BAZZILL; STAMP: WORDSWORTH

BRINGS HAPPINESS HAS NEVER
danced in the rain

BRINGS HAPPINESS HAS NEVER
danced in the rain

DANCED IN THE RAIN

• CREATE BACKGROUND BY ADHERING HALF A SHEET OF BLUE STRIPED PAPER TO WHITE CARDSTOCK • ADHERE A PIECE OF CIRCLE VELLUM ON TOP OF STRIPED PAPER WITH SCRAPPER SPRAY • ADHERE PHOTOS TO BACKGROUND • USE BLUE INK AND LETTER STAMPS FOR TITLE • ADHERE BITS AND BAUBLES FOR THE REST OF THE TITLE • STAMP NAME AND DATE ON CARDSTOCK AND SET IN WATCH CRYSTAL WITH GLASS BEADS • ADHERE CRYSTAL WITH DIAMOND GLAZE • HANG FIBERS FROM TOP OF LAYOUT TO RESEMBLE RAIN • HOLD FIBER DOWN WITH GLUE DOTS IN VARIOUS PLACES • MAKE THE SUN WITH TWISTAL • INK LAYOUT EDGES IN BLUE •
SUPPLIES – PRINTED VELLUM: SEI; STAMPS: PSX; 3-D EMBELLISHMENTS: CREATIVE IMAGINATIONS; FIBER: FIBERS BY THE YARD; TWISTAL: MAKING MEMORIES

GRANDSON

God gave me a special GIFT when you entered my LIFE.

With a bit of MISCHIEF and a twinkle in your eye, you GREET each day with OPEN arms.

You make me SMILE and bring me joy. Thank you for the GIFT of being my GRANDSON.

GRANDPA & JOSHUA 7-4-03

GRANDPA AND JOSHUA

• BEGIN WITH ORANGE CARDSTOCK FOR BACKGROUND • DOUBLE MAT LARGE PHOTO • TRIPLE MAT STRIP OF PHOTOS ALLOWING ROOM FOR TITLE ABOVE PHOTOS • ADHERE PHOTOS TO BACKGROUND • REVERSE PRINT TITLE AND DATE, CUT OUT AND ADHERE TO PHOTO MAT • PRINT JOURNALING ON VELLUM • DOUBLE MAT JOURNALING AND ADHERE TO BACKGROUND WITH SQUARE BRADS •
SUPPLIES – CARDSTOCK: BAZZILL; SQUARE BRADS: MAKING MEMORIES

A Mother's Love

Designer: Janet Hopkins

A Daughter Is...

• CREATE BACKGROUND BY ADHERING TORN PIECES OF GREEN AND PINK PATTERNED PAPER TO WHITE CARDSTOCK • TRIPLE MAT PHOTOS WITH CARDSTOCKS AND ADHERE TO BACK-GROUND • PRINT DAUGHTER POEM AND NAMES ON GREEN VELLUM • TEAR TOP AND BOTTOM EDGES • STAMP EDGES OF VELLUM AND HEAT EMBOSS WITH WHITE EMBOSSING POWDER • ADHERE TO LAYOUT • EMBELLISH LAYOUT WITH ROSE, SILVER PHOTO CORNERS AND DECORA-TIVE EYELETS • THREAD EYELETS WITH FIBERS • SUPPLIES - PATTERNED PAPER: LEISURE ARTS; METAL EMBELLISHMENTS: LEISURE ARTS; EYELETS: MAGIC SCRAPS

FROM THE HEART

• CREATE BACKGROUND BY ADHERING TORN FLORAL PAPER WITH CHALKED EDGES TO CARDSTOCK • MAT PHOTO WITH TORN CARDSTOCK AND FLORAL PAPER • COVER PHOTO WITH SWATCH OF TULLE FABRIC • ATTACH FABRIC WITH BRADS • PRINT JOURNALING ONTO PAPER AND MOUNT WITH FLORAL PAPER • WRAP JOURNALING WITH STRIPS OF ANTIQUED PAPER AND ADHERE TO PAGE • ANTIQUE SMALL ENVELOPE WITH STAIN AND RUBBER STAMPS • EMBELLISH LAYOUT WITH HEART CHARM, FIBERS AND A FAUX WAX SEAL • SUPPLIES – CARDSTOCK: BAZZILL; PATTERNED PAPERS: ANNA GRIFFIN, KAREN FOSTER; TULLE FABRIC: JOANN'S; ENVELOPE: TWO PEAS IN A BUCKET; FIBERS: ADORNMENTS; BRADS: BOXER; CHALKS: CRAF-T; STAMP: HERO ARTS, STAMPIN' UP; WAX SEAL: SONNETS

SPECIAL TIPS:

USE A GEL ANTIQUING MEDIUM INSTEAD OF WALNUT INK TO GIVE AN AGED LOOK. THE GEL IS EASIER TO USE AND NOT AS MESSY AS THE INK.

I am Your Mother

• BEGIN WITH BLACK CARDSTOCK FOR BACKGROUND • MAT PHOTO WITH PATTERNED PAPERS, BLACK AND WHITE CARDSTOCKS, AND TRANSPARENCY • ATTACH STICKERS FOR TITLE • TIE BOW AROUND ENTIRE LAYOUT • ATTACH METAL-RIMMED TAG WITH LETTER STICKERS TO RIBBON • EMBELLISH PHOTO WITH 'MOTHER' EYELET •
Supplies – Patterned Paper: Karen Foster, 7 Gypsies; Stickers: Sonnets; Eyelet Word: Making Memories

Love Being Your Mom

• CREATE BACKGROUND BY ADHERING TORN PATTERNED PAPER AND MESH TO BLUE CARDSTOCK • ADHERE PHOTOS TO LAYOUT • CREATE TITLE WITH LETTER STICKERS • BRUSH SMALL ENVELOPE WITH WALNUT INK AND ATTACH LETTER STICKERS • ATTACH ENVELOPE TO LAYOUT WITH HEMP • STAMP DATE AND ADHERE WITH MINI BRADS • ANTIQUE LOVE STICKER WITH WALNUT INK AND ADHERE TO LAYOUT •
Supplies – Paper: NRN Designs; Name Plate: NRN Designs; Mesh: Club Scrap; Stickers: NRN Designs, All the Extras, Making Memories; Date Stamp: Making Memories

IT'S ALL ABOUT

A Father's Love

Hand In Hand

- CREATE BACKGROUND BY ADHERING CORRUGATED CARDBOARD, PATTERNED PAPER, AND SAND PATTERNED PAPER TO BLACK CARDSTOCK
- DOUBLE MAT LARGE PHOTO
- SINGLE MAT ACCENT PHOTOS
- PRINT TITLE AND MAT ON CORRUGATED PAPER
- PRINT NAMES AND DATE AND ADHERE TO LAYOUT
- TWIST BLACK WIRE FOR ACCENT AND ADHERE TO LAYOUT
- Supplies – Patterned Paper: Paperbilities; Corrugated Paper: Paperbilities; Cardstock: Kraft

SPECIAL TIPS:
ADDING ACCENT PICTURES OF THE MAIN PHOTO IS A GREAT WAY TO USE YOUR DUPLICATE PHOTOS.

Hand in Hand...

Benjamin and Daddy   July 14, 2003

49

Daddy's Sweetheart

I am my daddy's sweetheart
He whispered it to me
But please don't tell my mommy
'Cause she used to be

I can already see a special bond forming between Alexandra and her Daddy.
It is so sweet when I am holding Alex and she catches a glimpse of her daddy.
Even if he is not looking at her, she gets the biggest smile on her face.
I am looking forward to seeing this bond grow even stronger over the years.

SPECIAL TIPS:
To give variety to a page, randomly change some photos from color to black and white.

Daddy's Sweetheart

• CREATE BACKGROUND BY CHALKING FLOWERS ONTO CARDSTOCK WITH A STENCIL • MAT PHOTO AND TEAR BOTTOM EDGE • USE SQUARE PUNCH TO CUT UNIFORM PHOTOS • CHALK EDGES OF TORN PHOTO MAT • PRINT TITLE AND JOURNALING ONTO CARDSTOCK • ADHERE PHOTOS TO CARDSTOCK • ATTACH PRINTED CARDSTOCKS TO BACKGROUND WITH EYELETS • EMBELLISH LAYOUT WITH FLOWER CHARMS AND EYELETS •
SUPPLIES – FONT: WORD ART, CHILLER; FLOWER CHARMS: MAKING MEMORIES; EYELETS: MAKING MEMORIES

A FatHeRs LOVE is FOREVER

Love Is Forever

• CREATE BACKGROUND BY ADHERING TORN HEART PATTERNED PAPER TO WHITE CARDSTOCK • ADHERE PHOTO TO BACKGROUND • TEAR LETTERS FOR 'LOVE' FREEHAND FROM HEART PATTERNED PAPER • ADHERE LETTER STICKERS AND TORN LETTERS TO LAYOUT FOR TITLE • CHALK ENTIRE LAYOUT WITH GREEN CHALK USING RANDOM STROKES • ADHERE WHITE FEATHER FIBERS TO LAYOUT • CHALK FIBERS WITH PINK CHALK • EMBELLISH LAYOUT WITH HEART CHARM •
SUPPLIES – PATTERNED PAPER: LEISURE ARTS; STICKERS: TREEHOUSE DESIGN; FIBER: FIBERS BY THE YARD

SPECIAL TIPS:
Use chalk to change the entire look of a layout if you don't have the right color cardstock.

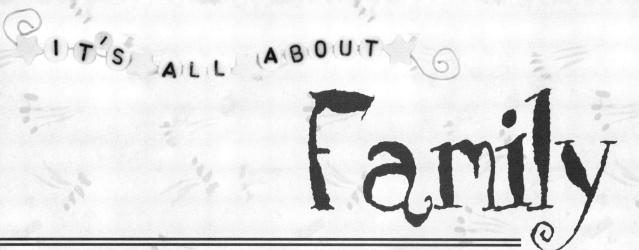

IT'S ALL ABOUT *Family*

WELCOME TO OUR WORLD

ellie

SISTERS

May 13, 2003

Designer: Camille Jensen

WELCOME TO OUR WORLD

• CREATE BACKGROUND BY ADHERING TORN STRIP OF PINK PATTERNED PAPER TOPPED WITH ROSEBUD PINK RIBBON TO YELLOW PATTERNED PAPER • WRAP PHOTOS WITH VARIEGATED EMBROIDERY FLOSS • ADHERE PHOTOS TO BACKGROUND • CREATE TITLE BY SEWING METAL LETTERS TO BACKGROUND WITH PINK FLOSS • ATTACH BUBBLE LETTERS TO LIGHT YELLOW MULBERRY PAPER AND MAT WITH PINK VELLUM AND GREEN MULBERRY PAPER • ATTACH 'SISTERS' ON FUN FOAM TO PINK HANDMADE PAPER, GREEN PATTERNED PAPER AND WHITE VELLUM • SEW TO LAYOUT WITH VARIEGATED GREEN FLOSS • MAT DATE STAMP WITH PINK HANDMADE PAPER AND YELLOW VELLUM AND ATTACH TO LAYOUT •
SUPPLIES – PATTERNED PAPER: LEISURE ARTS; METAL LETTER TAGS: DCWV; MULBERRY PAPER: DCWV

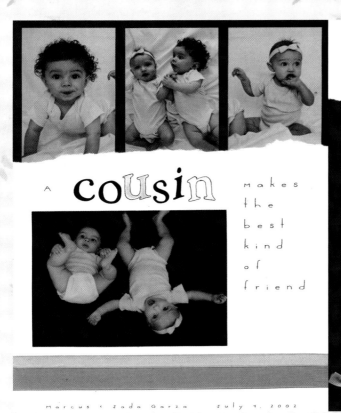

Marcus, not only are you and Jada cousins, you are good friends. When you're together you have to warm up to each other first and then the silliness begins. We all laughed as we took these photos of you two because Jada would get very excited and it would scare you or you would just grab her fingers and start biting away. I hope that you are always true friends and that you will look out for each other. That's what cousins & friends are for.

A **cousin** makes the best kind of friend

Marcus & Jada Garza   July 4, 2002

Designer: Emily Garza

COUSINS

- BEGIN WITH BLACK CARDSTOCK FOR BACKGROUND • ADHERE THREE PHOTOS TO BACKGROUND • MAT LARGER PHOTO WITH WHITE CARDSTOCK LEAVING ROOM FOR JOURNALING AND ADHERE TO BACKGROUND WITH TOP EDGE TORN • MAT THREE BLACK AND WHITE PHOTOS WITH WHITE CARDSTOCK • MAT COLOR PHOTO WITH PATTERNED PAPERS • ADHERE PHOTOS TO BACKGROUND • PRINT TITLE AND JOURNALING ON WHITE CARDSTOCK • USE ALPHABET STICKERS AND CHALK TO EMBELLISH TITLE • TEAR BOTTOM EDGE OF JOURNALING AND ADHERE TO LAYOUT • EMBELLISH LAYOUT WITH RIBBON AND CHARMS •

SUPPLIES – PATTERNED PAPER: ANNA GRIFFIN; STICKERS: CREATIVE IMAGINATIONS

SPECIAL TIPS:

1. WHEN YOU RUN OUT OF LETTER STICKERS USE THE STICKER SHEET AS A STENCIL. CHALK THE INSIDE OF THE STENCIL OR CUT OUT THE STENCIL, FRAMING THE EMPTY SPACE OF THE LETTER INSIDE AND USE IT AS A STICKER.
2. RUN RIBBON THROUGH A XYRON MACHINE FOR AN EASY WAY TO ADHERE IT TO A LAYOUT.

Since the day Ty was born, Matt has wanted to hold him. Matt finally had his chance. Ty is 6 weeks old in this picture. "Doesn't Matt look proud?"

Sept. 2003

HOLDING

HOLDING TY

- CREATE BACKGROUND BY ADHERING PATTERNED PAPERS, BLUE CARD-STOCK AND MESH TO TEXTURED CARDSTOCK • MAT PHOTO AND ADHERE TO PAGE • WRAP OTHER PHOTO WITH FELT AND STITCH AROUND EDGES • CREATE FIRST WORD OF TITLE WITH VELLUM STICKERS ON TEXTURED CARDSTOCK • STITCH TITLE BLOCK TO LAYOUT • FINISH TITLE BY CREAT-ING TAG WITH PATTERNED PAPER AND LETTER CHARMS • ATTACH TAG TO FELT WITH SAFETY PIN • PRINT JOURNALING ON VELLUM • ATTACH TO PAGE WITH CROSS-STITCHING • EMBELLISH LAYOUT WITH FIBERS •

SUPPLIES – CARDSTOCK: BAZZILL; PATTERNED PAPER: NRN DESIGNS, 7 GYPSIES; FLOSS: DMC; FIBERS: ADORNMENTS; MESH: MAGENTA; LETTER CHARMS: MAKING MEMORIES; TAG: AVERY; FONT: TWO PEAS IN A BUCKET RAGTAG

SPECIAL TIPS:

HOLD FABRIC IN PLACE WITH TEMPORARY ADHESIVE WHILE STITCHING AROUND A PHOTO.

Love Without
Measure

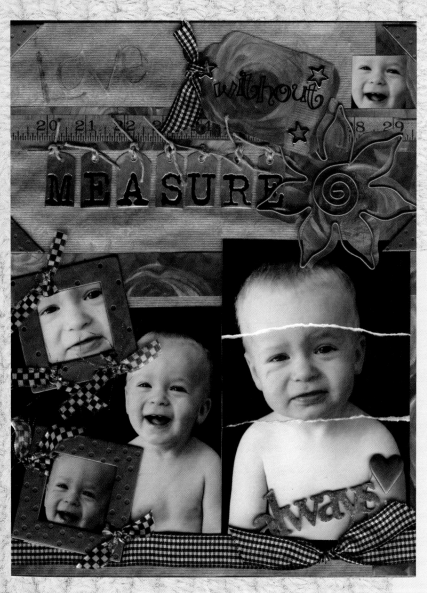

Always

- CREATE BACKGROUND BY ADHERING TEXTURED PAPER AND STRIPS OF FLORAL PAPER TO BLACK CARDSTOCK • ADHERE BLACK AND WHITE PHOTO TO BACKGROUND • MAKE BLACK AND WHITE AND COLOR COPY OF OTHER PHOTO • ADHERE COLORED PHOTO TO BACKGROUND • TEAR CENTER SECTION FROM BLACK AND WHITE PHOTO AND ADHERE ATOP COLORED PHOTO • CUT TWO SQUARE PHOTOS AND ADHERE TO SQUARE METAL FRAMES (USE PORTION OF TORN PHOTO FOR ONE FRAME) • CREATE TITLE WITH 'LOVE' TEMPLATE AND CHALK WITH RED AND BLACK CHALK • PRINT 'WITHOUT' ON TRANSPARENCY AND ADHERE TO TAG MADE FROM PATTERNED PAPERS • ATTACH TAG TO LAYOUT WITH THREE STAR CONCHES AND GINGHAM RIBBON • ATTACH EYELET METAL LETTERS TO LAYOUT WITH HEMP • HEAT EMBOSS 'ALWAYS' LETTER WITH RED EMBOSSING POWDER AND ADHERE TO LAYOUT • EMBELLISH LAYOUT WITH HEART EYELET, GINGHAM RIBBON, PHOTO CORNERS, MEASURING TAPE STICKER AND METAL FLOWER PAPER CLIP •

SUPPLIES – PATTERNED PAPER: ANNA GRIFFIN; METAL FRAMES: MAKING MEMORIES, METAL WORD: MAKING MEMORIES; HEART EYELET: MAKING MEMORIES; RIBBON: MICHAELS; PHOTO CORNERS: MAKING MEMORIES; STICKERS: REBECCA SOWER; EYELET LETTERS: MAKING MEMORIES; PIER ONE; LETTER TEMPLATE: MAKING MEMORIES

Designer: Jan Zondros

THE WORLD

• BEGIN WITH MAP PATTERNED PAPER FOR BACKGROUND • MAT PHOTOS • PRINT TITLE ON TRANSPARENCY • FINISH TITLE WITH LETTER STICKERS • ADHERE TRANSPARENCY WITH CLEAR DOUBLE-SIDED TAPE • EMBELLISH WITH BOTTLE AND SHIP WHEEL •

Supplies – Patterned Paper: Sonnets; Stickers: Sonnets; Bottle: Jolee's Boutique; Ships Wheel: Dress it Up; Font: Two Peas in a Bucket Dreams

SPECIAL TIPS:

Use a transparency for printing titles and journaling when you have a pretty piece of paper to show through and don't want it covered by journal boxes.

To the world you might be just one person. But to one person you just might be the World

CHILDREN ARE THE KEY TO PARADISE

• CREATE BACKGROUND BY ADHERING TORN AND DISTRESSED PIECE OF PATTERNED PAPER TO ANTIQUE KEY PAPER • TEAR EDGES OF PHOTO AND INK • TEAR, CRUMPLE, SAND AND INK SMALLER PHOTO • CREATE TITLE WITH AN ASSORTMENT OF LETTER WORDS • ATTACH KEY MAGNETS WITH FIBER AND SILVER BRADS • FRAME TITLE BOX WITH FIBER •

Supplies – Paper: SEI; Fiber: Fiber by the Yard; Brads: Making Memories; Key Magnets: Target; Letters: Wordsworth, Sonnets, Making Memories, Rebecca Sower

LETTER TO MY DAUGHTER SOPHIA

• CREATE BACKGROUND BY ADHERING FLORAL PAPER AND WORD PATTERNED PAPER TO GREEN CARDSTOCK • MAT LARGE PHOTO WITH TWILL TAPE • ADHERE PHOTOS TO LAYOUT • ATTACH TWILL TAPE TO LOWER CORNER OF SMALL PHOTO • ADHERE FRAME OVER SMALLER PHOTO SKEWED TO ONE SIDE • PRINT TEXT ON SMALL PIECE OF VELLUM AND TEAR • INK EDGES OF VELLUM WITH PINK INK • ATTACH VELLUM TAG TO OPEN CARD WITH EYELETS • CREATE CARD FROM CRAFT PAPER AND ADHERE TORN PIECE OF FLORAL PAPER TO CORNER OF CARD • CREATE WAX SEAL BY MELTING A COLORED GLUE STICK ONTO A SCRAP PIECE OF CARDSTOCK • STAMP WAX WITH DESIRED STAMP • HANDWRITE PRIVATE LETTER AND SLIDE INSIDE CARD • GLUE BACK OF CARD TO LAYOUT • EMBELLISH WITH CLIP, RUB-ON WORDS AND RIBBON •

Supplies – Twill Tape: 7 Gypsies; Rub-on Words: Making Memories

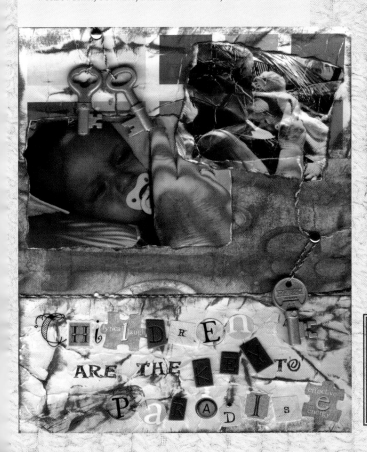

SPECIAL TIPS:

Sepia stamp ink is an excellent way to "antique" a layout without the mess of walnut ink.

IT'S ALL ABOUT
Ties That Bind

Designer: Peggy Manrique

GROWING CLOSER

• CREATE BACKGROUND BY ADHERING STRIPS OF STRIPE, COLLAGE AND CRUMPLED RED LINEN PAPER TO CARDSTOCK • RUB RED PAPER WITH BROWN INK TO DEFINE WRINKLES • ADD THE DATE TO THE PHOTO, PRINT ONTO WHITE CARD-STOCK AND ADHERE PHOTO TO BACKGROUND • CREATE TITLE WITH LETTERING STICKERS • ATTACH LETTER STICKERS TO TAGS FOR JOURNALING • STRING TAGS WITH BROWN GINGHAM RIBBON AND ADHERE TO PAGE • EMBELLISH LAY-OUT WITH BROTHER AND SISTER WISDOM STICKERS, CIRCLE CLIPS AND SILVER HINGES •

Supplies – Cardstock: Bazzill; Patterned Paper: Chatterbox, Legacy Collage, K & Company; Stickers: Nostalgique, Scrapbook Stickerz; Circle Clips: Making Memories; Silver Hinges: Making Memories

Computer Education:

THE SKY IS THE LIMIT WHEN COMPUTERS AND THE INTERNET ARE USED IN SCRAPBOOKING. HERE ARE SOME WAYS YOU CAN USE THE COMPUTER TO IMPROVE YOUR LAYOUTS.

THE FONTS USED FOR TITLES AND JOURNALING CAN CHANGE THE ENTIRE FEEL OF A LAYOUT. THERE IS AN ENDLESS SUPPLY OF FONTS TO CHOOSE FROM ON THE COMPUTER. THEY CAN BE FOUND IN WORD PROCESSING PROGRAMS, OTHER PURCHASED SOFTWARE PROGRAMS AND THE INTERNET. MANY INTERNET SITES PROVIDE FREE DOWNLOADABLE FONTS OR PURCHASABLE FONTS. TRY USING MANY DIFFERENT FONTS ON ONE LAYOUT TO DRAW ATTENTION TO YOUR TEXT.

PRINT TEXT IN VARYING SIZES AND COLORS WITH ITALICS, BOR-DERS AND BOLD LETTERING TO ADD INTEREST TO A LAYOUT. LAYER TEXT BOXES TO ADD DIMENSION AND CREATE BACK-GROUNDS TO ADD TEXTURE. HIGHLIGHT WORDS WITH COLOR, FONT AND SIZE.

ALTER DIGITAL OR SCANNED PHOTOS WITH PHOTO SOFTWARE PROGRAMS. THE COLOR OF A PHOTO CAN BE CHANGED FROM COLOR TO BLACK AND WHITE OR SEPIA. THE SHAPE AND SIZE OF THE PHOTO CAN BE ADJUSTED TO FIT THE LAYOUT. SOFTWARE PROGRAMS CAN LAYER PHOTOS, ADJUST COLOR TONES, CHANGE THE TEXTURE OF A PHOTO AND PRINT JOUR-NALING ONTO THE PHOTOS AS WELL. THE MEDIUM ON WHICH PHOTOS ARE PRINTED CAN AFFECT THE LOOK OF THE PHOTO AS WELL. TRY PRINTING ONTO PHOTO PAPER, REGULAR PAPER, CANVAS, VELLUM, TRANSPARENCIES, AND OTHER MEDIUMS.

SCANNING PHOTOS AND IMAGES INTO A COMPUTER OPENS NEW POSSIBILITIES FOR THE SCRAPBOOKER. PHOTOS CAN BE ALTERED WITH A PHOTO SOFTWARE PROGRAM, SENT TO FRIENDS OVER THE INTERNET, ETC. IT IS MOST COMMON TO SAVE PHOTOS AS A JPEG FILE BECAUSE THEY ARE EASIER TO SAVE, REQUIRE LESS STORAGE SPACE AND ARE EASIER TO SEND OVER THE INTERNET. PHOTOS CAN ALSO BE SAVED AS EPS, TIFF OR PICT FILES. A SCANNED PHOTO CAN BE SAVED TO WHATEVER SIZE DESIRED. JUST REMEMBER THAT IT TAKES SOME PATIENCE AND WORK TO GET THE SAME COLOR TONES YOU SEE ON YOUR SCREEN TO APPEAR ON THE PRINTED PHOTO.

THERE ARE MANY DIFFERENT GRAPHICS AVAILABLE TO THE SCRAPBOOK AND PAPER ARTIST. CLIP ART AND OTHER GRAPH-ICS ARE WIDELY AVAILABLE ON THE INTERNET. MOST GRAPHICS COME WITH A SET OF INSTRUCTIONS ON HOW TO USE THEM AND SHOULD BE AVAILABLE TO BOTH IBM COMPATIBLE AND MACINTOSH USERS. THERE ARE SOME AMAZING PRODUCTS AVAILABLE, JUST BE SURE TO READ THE FINE PRINT BEFORE PUR-CHASING PRODUCTS.

evolving as
brothers

guide   learn   love

laugh   share   play

We are so lucky to have you boys as our sons. Watching your relationship bloom into what it is today has been a beautiful, wonderful, gradual, natural evolution. Michael, you were our only child for 3 1/2yrs. We knew that baby Hunter would take some getting used to. We tried not to rush you, having faith that your feelings of indifference would eventually fade into genuine affection on its own, given time and space. It seems we were right.... You two boys are so crazy about eachother now. You love to play together- laughing, loving, wrestling... being boys, being brothers. Everyone warned us that there would be jealousy between you... so far that has never been an issue. I know the day will come when you boys will squabble & disagree... but for now I will cherish every shared smile, giggle, hug, kiss, and reassuring embrace.

Designer: Renee Villalobos-Campa

EVOLVING AS BROTHERS

• CREATE BACKGROUND BY ADHERING TRIMMED CARDSTOCK STAMPED WITH SHADOW INK TO BLACK CARDSTOCK • TRIM NINE PHOTOS TO DESIRED SIZE AND MAT WITH BLACK CARDSTOCK • ADHERE PHOTOS TO BACKGROUND LEAVING 1\2" BORDER BETWEEN EACH PHOTO • MAT TWO PHOTOS WITH WHITE CARDSTOCK AND DOUBLE MAT LARGE PHOTO WITH JOURNALING • REVERSE PRINT TITLE AND SUPPORTING WORDS • CUT OUT AND ADHERE TITLE TO BLACK CARDSTOCK • PRINT JOURNAL BLOCK AND HIGHLIGHT KEY WORDS WITH A PEN • ADHERE PHOTOS AND TITLE TO LAYOUT •

SUPPLIES – STAMPS: HERO ARTS, STAMPABILITIES, PAPER INSPIRATIONS; FONT: AMAZON BT

dEar DawSon & aBbi

I often don't feel like I live up to the wonderful name by which you call me, Mommy. I find myself wondering each night how I can be a better Mommy the next day. Many times I succeed and other times I feel I fell short of my responsibilities. But one thing is always for certain, I adore you both with all my heart and would do anything for you.

You are growing up much too quickly so I thought I'd take this opportunity to express my love for each you. My love for you is unconditional, it is never ending and it will always be that way.

Dawson, I love your big loves and kisses that are always presented to me at just the right moment, sometimes unexpected but always very welcome. And Abbi, I love how you say 'Ma' repeatedly until you have my complete and undivided attention. You have also learned that giving loves and kisses is the way we express ourselves.

Another favorite thought that comes to my mind is when you both decide to lay atop my tummy as I attempt to do my morning exercises and sit-ups–fighting for the chance to give me the best love or kiss.

So I want to thank you for being patient with me while I learn all about each of you and your attributes and each day I promise to learn something new that I can carry into tomorrow and make even better days for us in the future! I love you more than you could possibly comprehend.

Loving you both dearly,

MommY

DEAR DAWSON AND ABBI

• BEGIN WITH STRIPE PATTERNED PAPER FOR BACKGROUND • PUNCH OUT FOUR PHOTOS WITH SQUARE PUNCH • DOUBLE MAT MAIN PHOTO AND RUN GINGHAM RIBBON ALONG BOTTOM OF MAT • PRINT JOURNALING AND MAT WITH GINGHAM RIBBON ALONG TOP • ADHERE ELEMENTS TO BACKGROUND • EMBELLISH WITH METAL-RIMMED TAGS AND STRING •

SUPPLIES – PATTERNED PAPER: AMERICAN CRAFTS; STAMP: HERO ARTS

Our Designers Favorite Tools

Creating a great scrapbook page can become a whole lot easier if you have the right tools and equipment. We asked some of our best designers to give us a list of the scrapbooking tools they could not live without. Here is their list:

1. CARDSTOCK
2. EMBOSSING POWDER
3. PAPER TRIMMER
4. EYELET TOOL
5. SEWING MACHINE
6. DECORATIVE SCISSORS
7. CHALK
8. HERMAFIX
9. HOLE PUNCHES

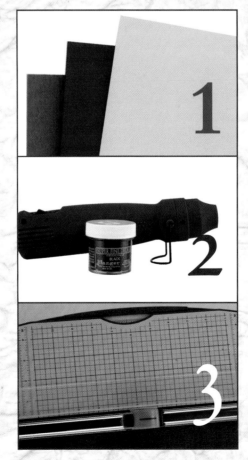

And Scrapbooking Tips

Paper Curling

Add dimension to your scrap-booking pages with curled paper. Just wet the edges of torn paper with a cotton swab and gently roll paper with your fingers. Let the paper dry and it will stay curled. Paper curling is easy to do and a great way to use single and double sided paper and cardstock. Add variety to your paper curling by layering paper curls and framing photos and journaling.

Fabric

Incorporate fabric into your layouts to add dimension, texture and interest to your pages. The color and texture of fabric help set the theme of a layout and make the viewer want to touch the page. Try using some of the following fabrics in your next scrap-booking page:

- Felt
- Vinyl
- Netting
- Denim
- Velvet
- Corduroy

Stitching

Try stitching on your scrapbook pages with a needle and thread or sewing machine. Stitching gives a finishing touch to your pages that shows attention to detail and makes the entire layout look even better. Add any stitches you can think of as a border, frame, decoration, or even to attach elements together. Here are some other ideas:

- Stitch letters to create words or decorations
- Use a straight, zig-zag or vine stitch for a border
- Stitch designs to embellish layout
- Use cross stitches to adhere element to background
- Thread beads, charms and tags to background

Sources

The following companies manufacture products featured in this book. Please check with your local retail store for these materials. We have made every attempt to identify and give proper credit for the materials used in this book. If, by chance, we have missed giving the appropriate credit, we would appreciate hearing from you.

3L Corp.
(800) 828-3130 3lcorp.com

3M Stationary
(800) 364-3577 3m.com

7-Gypsies
(800) 588 6707 7gypsies.com

Adornments
adornments.com

American Craft
(800) 642-4314 americancraft.com

American Tag Company
(800) 223-3956 americantag.net

Anna Griffin, Inc.
(888) 817-8170 annagriffin.com

Avery
(800) GO-AVERY avery.com

Bazzill Basics Paper
(480) 558-8557 bazzillbasics.com

Bluemoon Beads
(800) 377-6715 bluemoonbeads.com

Brown Bag Fibers
brownbagfibers.com

Boxer Scrapbook Productions, LLC
(888) 625-6255 or (503) 625-0455 boxer-scrapbooks.com

Carolee's Creations
(435) 563-1100 caroleescreations.com

Clearsnap
(888) 448-4862 clearsnap.com

Club Scrap
(888) 634-9100 clubscrap.com

Coats & Clark
coatsandclark.com

Creative Imaginations
(800) 942-6487 cigift.com

Daisy D's Paper Co.
(888) 601-8955 or (801) 447-9955 daisydotsanddoodles.com

Deluxe Cuts
(480) 497-9005 deluxecuts.com

DieCuts with a View
(801) 224-6766 diecutswithaview.com

DMC
(973) 589-0606 dmc-usa.com

DMD Industries
(800) 805-9890 dmdind.com

Dress It Up
dressitup.com

DYMO
(800) 426-7827 dymo.com

Eclectic Products, Inc.
(800) 767-4667 eclecticproucts.com

EK Success
(800) 524-1349 eksuccess.com

Ellison
(800) 253-2240 ellison.com

Embellish It
(702) 312-1628 embellishit.com

Family Treasures
(661) 294-1330 familytreasures.com

Fibers by the Yard
fibersbytheyard.com

Flavia
(805) 882-2466 flavia.com

Herma Fix
Herma.co.uk.com

Hero Art Rubber Stamps, Inc.
(800) 822-4376 hearoarts.com

Jest Charming
(702) 564-5101 jestcharming.com

Jones Tones
(719) 948-0048 jonestones.com

Junkitz
(212) 944-4250 junitz.com

Junque
Junque.net

K & Company
(888) 244-2083 kandcompany.com

Kangaroo & Joey
(480) 460-4841 kangarooandjoey.com

Karen Foster Design
(801) 451-9779 karenfosterdesign.com

Leisure Arts
(888) 257-7548 business.leisurearts.com

Making Memories
(800) 286-5263 makingmemories.com

Mrs. Grossman's
(800) 429-4549 mrsgrossmans.com

National Cardstock
(724) 452-7120 nationalcardstock.com

NRN Designs
nrndesigns.com

Paper Garden
papergarden.com

Paper Illuzionz
(406) 234-8716 paperilluzionz.com

Provo Craft
(888) 577-3545 provocraft.com

PSX Design
(800) 782-6748 psxdesign.com

Quickutz
(888) 702-1146 quickutz.com

ScrapLovers
scraplovers.com

Scrapworks, LLC
scrapworksllc.com

Sculpey
Sculpey.com

SEI, Inc.
(800) 333-3279 shopsei.com

Stampin' Up!
(800) 782-6787 stampinup.com

Stickopotamus
(888) 270-4443 stickopotamus.com

Timeless Touches
(623) 362-8285 timelesstouches.net

Treehouse Designs
(877) 372-1109 treehouse-designs.com

Two Peas In A Bucket
twopeasinabucket.com

TwoTwinkles.Com
(760) 961-2500 twotwinkles.com

Un-Du
Un-du.com

Westrim Crafts
(800) 727-2727 westrimcrafts.com

Words Worth Stamps
(719) 282-3495 wordsworthstamps.com

Xyron
(800) 793-3523 xyron.com

Look for these published or soon to be published
                              Leisure Arts Scrapbooking Idea Books

IT'S ALL IN YOUR IMAGINATION

IT'S ALL ABOUT SCHOOL

IT'S ALL ABOUT TECHNIQUE

IT'S ALL ABOUT CARDS AND TAGS

IT'S ALL ABOUT PETS

IT'S ALL ABOUT TRAVEL

IT'S ALL ABOUT THE PAST

IT'S ALL ABOUT TEENS

IT'S ALL ABOUT STEP-SAVING DESIGNS